# 88+ Ways

# *MUSIC*

## Can Change

# *Your Life*

D1408904

"88+ Ways Music Can Change Your Life"

Written by Vincent James & Joann Pierdomenico

Keep Music Alive
www.KeepMusicAlive.org
www.facebook.com/KeepMusicAliveMission
@88WaysMusic


ISBN: 978-0998363707


Printed in the U.S.A

# Forward

*People always ask me why we never did a "Chicken Soup for the Musician's Soul" and now you've done it! I love this book... the title, the cover, I love what's in it.*

*Music is very dear to me and my kids, and it's very unfortunate what's happening in this country with music education. Every music teacher in America should be giving "88+ Ways" to their students. It would really give them inspiration, not only in terms of music, but in terms of living your dreams. Just read it!*

**Jack Canfield** - Co-creator/author of the "Chicken Soup for the Soul"® series and author of "The Success Principles"™

# Table of Contents

## Inspiration & Motivation

Remembering You Today - Adam Ezra w/Bruce Fredericks ..............3
Never Give Up! - Audra Mclaughlin ...............................7
Music = Emotion - Audrey Landers ...............................9
3 Kinds of People - Baran ......................................11
Like A Virgin - Billy Steinberg................................12
Living Your Life for Happiness - Bobby Kimball.................15
Thanks Mom - Bonnie Warren ....................................17
Making Mom Happy Again - Bronsen Bloom ........................18
The Amazing Avah Grace - Connie Kerbs .........................19
Music Saved Me from Myself - Derek Anthony Wilson..............24
A Divine Gift From the Universe - Erin Carere .................26
Standing on the Shoulders - Fred Mollin........................28
The Path of a Professional Musician - Gary Alexander...........31
Saved by the Guitar - Gregg Hammond ...........................34
The Decision Chair - Hank Alviani.............................36
Together for Just One Night - Jana Mashonee ..................39
I Don't Believe in Plan B - Jay Gruska .......................41
Connecting From the Heart - Jessica Lynn .....................43
Never Believe Them - JKELL....................................45
If You Don't Dream Big, Why Dream At All - Joey James.........45
It's Not All Unicorns and Rainbows - Jordan White ............47
Maybe It's You - Judy Pancoast ...............................49
Don't Give Up - Kelsey Coan ..................................50
Birth of an Artist - Kevin Vieira ............................53
Kids for the Blues - Krista Hughes & Eve Bare ................58
Best and Most Beautiful Things in Life - Kristin Smedley......61
Above Water - Melissa Polinar ................................63
Breaking Down - Mini Thin ....................................65
The Greatest Gift One Could Ever Give - Rick Wakeman .........65
In Honor of My Brothers - Ryan Weaver.........................66

# Inspiration & Motivation

Man in the Mirror - Siedah Garrett.................................68
When Words Fail, Music Speaks - Simon Kirke ...........70
You Get What You Give - Taylor Abrahamse ...............72
Penny Shouts It Out! - Theresa Shoup........................76
Every Note and Lyric - Valerie West.............................80
Music is Magic - Vanessa Carlton...............................80
Hop & Pull - Wolfgang Gowin......................................81
It Takes a Village - Yosmar Salazar-Márquez Vinson....83
The Gift of Music - Ziba Shirazi ..................................86

# Musical Memories

One Note at a Time - Andre Maranhao .........................89
Best Education I Ever Received - Bluesman Jay Gullo....91
Anyone Here Play the Banjo? - Bobby Hart & Glenn Ballantyne.......94
Who Sings That Song? - Chris D'Antonio .....................97
Unforgettable - David Charles......................................98
The World of Harry Chapin - Howard Fields...................99
Changing the Course of History - Leon Jordan, Sr..........101
Feel the Magic in Your Life - Michel Rubini ................102
Hard Days, Hard Nights - Pat DiCesare ....................106
There's Always a Song - Rob Hyman ..........................110
Classical Fab-Four Inspires Some Funky Music - Rob Parissi........113
What I Did for Love - Rose Kingsley............................114
Million to One - Skip Denenberg ................................117
On the Mic - Steve Kurtz............................................119

# Music & Education

*A Day to Remember at Claremont Elementary - The Battersbys* ....122
*Keep Your Ears Open - Craig Snyder* ........................................123
*Dorothy Cho: Warrior of Hope - Khim Teoh* ..............................125
*HOME - Jasmine Mya Yedra* .................................................129
*Keep Music Alive - Marcy Holub* ............................................133
*How Marching Band Changed My Life at Age 40! - Matthew Keith* ..135
*I Teach People, Not Pianos - Nick Ambrosino* ...........................137
*A Hidden Star - Patricia Shih* ...............................................139
*An Open Letter to All School Superintendents - Peter P. Carli II* .....141

# Music & Healing

*The Jazz Sanctuary - Alan Segal* ............................................147
*I Truly Could Not Live a Day - Ann Kelly* ..................................147
*The Living Years - Bill Champlin* ............................................149
*Music Will Never Give Up on Us - Chris McDermott* .....................149
*A Whisper Heard Around The World - Dalton Cyr* ........................152
*My Guardian Angel - Darcy Donavan* ......................................153
*We're All in This Together - Dr. Deb Carlin* ...............................155
*Play Your Own Therapy - Elise Hofmann* ..................................158
*The Better You Get, The More You'll Enjoy It - Eric Jacobsen* ........160
*The Biggest Reward - Grace Otley* ..........................................162
*To All Purple Tree Trunks - Jack Pearson* .................................164
*Singing for Baby - Julia Zane* ................................................165
*The Power to Heal - Katherine Dines* .......................................166
*Music is My Lifeline & I Can't Stop Creating - Lisa Sniderman* .......168
*The Power of Music - Mark King* .............................................173
*Music Brought My Mother Back to Me - Miguel Sague* .................174
*A Quiet, Driving Force Inside of Me - Pete Shand* .......................176
*Therapy for the Performer Too - Phyllis Chapell* .........................178
*Marching Beyond Halftime - Sara Flatow* ..................................179
*Heaven's Gate - Sara Spicer* .................................................182
*How I Found the Real Me - Suzanne Gorman* ............................184

# Music & Healing

Music Lifts Us, When Nothing Else Can - Suzi Shelton ...............186
Forever Gone But Never Forgotten - Veronica Kole ....................188
No Matter What, Write a Song About It - Victoria De Mare ...........190
Will I Be Able to Play the Guitar Ever Again? - Warren Golden ......191

# Musical Potpourri

Music & Love - 6StringSarch ....................................196
Getaway - Alex B .................................................196
Nothing to Fear - Aly Spaltro of Lady Lamb ......................197
We ARE the Music - Andy Mason ...................................198
A Song In Your Heart - Bonnie Thomas ............................198
We Remember - Brian Maes ........................................199
Dear Music - Brooke Falls .......................................200
If You Can't Find the Right Words - Buddy Brown .................201
He Ain't Heavy, He's My Brother - Carol Blackman ...............202
Like an Old Friend - Ciaran Gribbin ............................204
We Can't All Be Playing - Cindy Barry Strobel ..................206
Surf and Sound Make Beautiful Music - Cody Lovaas ..............207
My Most Treasured Instrument - Debbie Wiseman ..................208
Music is My Smile - Desireless .................................208
An Unconscious Process - Eric Bazilian ........................209
Optimum Results - Errol Desmond LeBlanc .......................211
Every Piece of Human Emotion - Gary Mallaber ..................211
Hard to Say Goodbye - Great White .............................212
The Common Thread that Binds Us All - Jeff Oster ..............213
Just One Song - Luis Souza ....................................214
In Tune with Life - Mike Kalombo .............................216
How I Got Back to Music - Ray Naylor .........................216
Why Music Matters to Me – Joann Pierdomenico .................219

Story Index by Contributor Name .............................226

# Introduction

The stories you will read in "88+ Ways Music Can Change Your Life" come from "deep down" in those who have written them. For some, it was painstakingly difficult to put into writing and even more so to share. For others, the experience was a form of therapy... writing helped them heal from their own situations and even prompted some to reach out to people they haven't seen or spoken to in many years. Some stories were whipped out in a matter of minutes, whereas, others took hours, days and even weeks to put together. However their stories and quotes came to be, "88+ Ways" would like to say "Thank You" to each and every contributor for their time, effort and support of "Keep Music Alive". Without you, our contributors, "88+ Ways" could not be the emotional and inspiring book that it has come to be.

There are stories that will really make you think, some that will make you laugh and, yes, a number of them will bring you to tears. Our hope, is that they will inspire and help you to remember the beauty and power of music.

# Dedication

To my amazing wife, Joann:

You have supported me with your love and inspiration throughout my many musical adventures over the last 25 years. Too many times while I was off in recording studios, promoting events, managing other artists or performing myself, you were at home (almost single-handedly) raising our family. When I asked you to be my co-author for "88+ Ways", I prayed that your answer would be YES and that we would finally get to work on a music project together again. Thankfully, you answered my prayers, as you have done in every other aspect of my life. You are my true soulmate... my life could never be the same without you.

~Vincent

# *Inspiration*
# *&*
# *Motivation*

"I BELIEVE I CAN FLY - I BELIEVE I CAN
TOUCH THE SKY....."

*Sometimes, the only thing holding
us back is our own beliefs.*

## "Remembering You Today"

We were touring through New Jersey and Pennsylvania when I got a call from a guy named Jerry. He said his friend, Terri, was a huge fan who was currently losing her battle with cancer. She was too sick to come out to a show, and he asked if I could possibly stop by her house and visit with her for a bit. I didn't know Jerry or Terri, but decided to have the band drop me off in Jersey on their way back home to Boston so I could show up at Terri's house for a surprise visit.

I got to the house and Terri's husband, Bruce, met me at the door. He looked nervous. I walked in and there were friends and family milling around. They all looked nervous too. Terri was upstairs in bed. She hadn't gotten out of bed in days. She hadn't eaten in days. Things were pretty bad.

I sat down and made small talk for a while with some of Terri's friends, and after a bit, Bruce came down and told me she was ready for me to come see her. I grabbed my guitar and went up the stairs. I walked into the room and this very pale, frail woman was lying in a hospital bed. She looked listless. When I leaned over the bed, she opened her eyes and smiled at me. She had a beautiful smile, even in the midst of her suffering.

I said, "Hey Terri. Would you like me to play you a song?" She nodded yes. I began to play a slow, quiet song. She closed her eyes and smiled as I played. When I finished, I said, "another?" She smiled and nodded yes. After about three songs, she said, "I think I'm ready to go downstairs now." Bruce and Terri's friend, Rachelle, helped lift Terri out of bed and brought her downstairs to a couch in the living room where friends and family were gathered, waiting reverently for Terri to join them. They sat her on the couch, propped up with pillows. I sat next to her and asked her for a request. I forget which song she chose, but when I finished, she requested another.

Five to six songs in, she began to sing along.

Eight to ten songs in, she asked for some food. An hour after that, she asked for seconds.

She began telling stories of how she and Bruce met. Terri was funny!

We spent six precious, unexpected, hours... all of us singing, laughing, and crying together. Terri died later that week. I still remain in awe of the incredible experience we all shared that day and still think about her often.

*Adam Ezra*
*The Adam Ezra Group*
*www.AdamEzra.com*

**BONUS** - *What follows is a beautiful narrative from Terri's husband, Bruce, about their experience with Adam*

We first heard the Adam Ezra Group (AEG) on a family ski vacation in New Hampshire. We all loved the music and bought the CD. Since we live in New Jersey, we figured it was unlikely we would get to see them again, being so far from their home base of Boston. Time passed and about 3 ½ years into Terri's breast cancer, she saw that Adam was coming to the World Café Live in Philly. We grabbed our friends, Rachelle and Wayne, caught the show and immediately remembered why we fell in love with Adam's music. Terri and Rachelle talked about bringing AEG to play at a friend's barn and even contacted Adam's agent to start working the details. Unfortunately, after many ups and downs over 5+ years of breast cancer, Terri was on a painful decline. In November of 2013, we heard that Adam and his group were coming to a bar very close to us. But Terri's decline was continuing. As it got closer, I put the word out to friends and family to go and see Adam for us and bring Terri's love and spirit. What I didn't know was that my longtime friend, Jerry, had contacted Adam and asked if he would stop by to see Terri the day after his show. I'm still amazed to say that Adam agreed without hesitation.

The Sunday after the show, I gathered about a dozen close friends and family to be part of Adam's visit. Unfortunately, Terri was in excruciating pain that entire day. When Adam showed up, I quickly explained the situation. At that time, Terri was upstairs and had 3 people working on her, constantly, for hours trying to alleviate her pain and bring comfort. She could barely communicate. Waiting downstairs, Adam kept saying, "no problem - I have all day; take your time".

I had not told Terri that Adam was coming, so I went to the bedroom and whispered in her ear that Adam Ezra was downstairs and wanted to say hello. She closed her eyes and became very still. After a moment, she quietly said, "ask him to come up in 15 minutes". About 20 minutes later, Terri's best friend, Rachelle, came downstairs and asked Adam to come up. Guitar in hand, Adam climbed the steps and quietly entered the room. Terri almost instantly went from her painful state, to a quiet, relaxed calm. She smiled softly as Adam spoke to her and held her hand. Adam played several songs as Terri became more and more at ease; the soft smile remained on her face and gradually overtook her whole body.

After a few songs upstairs, Terri asked to be carried downstairs where we sat together for six hours! Adam played every song Terri asked for. At one point, Terri asked Adam to play a sing-a-long. This was amazing, because Terri had not sung with me for well over a year saying that the cancer had made it too difficult. Now, here she was, only days before her passing and she was actually singing along with Adam.

The day continued as we sat around and talked about all sorts of things with Adam, as if we'd known him all our lives. Then, Adam provided the most beautiful gift Terri and I could receive. He began to draw out of us, the story of how we met and fell in love. As Terri and I recounted it, it brought us back to the feelings that drew us together in the beginning. And we remembered, again, how we actually had a true "lightning bolt moment". At that moment, it completely shifted our relationship and interactions from "caregiver and patient" to "head over heels in love husband and wife".

Terri's process of death and transition was a beautiful love filled process. This man who did not even know us, brought Terri and all of us to the right place with his generous loving soul and heartfelt talented music. All the friends and family who were there have been changed forever by this experience, and I am forever indebted to Adam for his gift. As everyone thanked him that day, he responded to each that it was he who got so much more that day than he gave.

Since then, Adam has written a song called "You Today" that beautifully captures the feelings of that day (to listen please search "Adam Ezra" and "You Today" on YouTube). I encourage everyone to support Adam and artists everywhere who pour their hearts and souls into their craft so that all our lives can shine a little brighter, making some of our most difficult times more bearable. Thank you, Adam Ezra, from the bottom of my heart.

*Bruce Fredericks*
*Pennington, New Jersey – U.S.A.*

*The Adam Ezra Group is currently touring and playing grassroots charity events through Adam's non-profit organization "RallySound". To find out more, please visit: www.AdamEzra.com*

## "*Never Give Up!*"

Academically, I struggled all through school, and found it very difficult to keep up with my classmates. I ended up being placed in separate classes with about 6 other students. I wanted so badly to fit in with the popular kids, but instead, I always felt singled out. Many times, I remember walking down the hallway and kids would call me stupid and other hateful words. I constantly felt like an easy target and as a result, had very low self-esteem throughout my school years. I let everything and everyone bring me down. Many days, I would come home crying to my mom, because I just wished school was easier for me. I would tell myself I would never accomplish anything in life. What I had yet to discover, was that I needed to start believing in myself.

For my first year of high-school, I wanted to have a fresh start, so I asked to be put in regular classes. I thought that if I tried hard enough, I would be able to keep up. Half way into the year, I was failing most of my subjects. I was then placed in classes where there were 2 teachers and a few other students and the cycle of low-esteem continued. Music was, ultimately, where I ended up turning to cope with my emotions. What's interesting, is that when I finally went off to college, I was able to finish with a 3.5 grade point average. This was an amazing accomplishment for me and was only possible due to the confidence I had gained through my involvement in music. By this point, I knew without a doubt, that SINGING was what I was destined to do in life.

I had many musical influences while growing up, beginning with my grandpop, who is now 85 years old and has been singing and playing the piano by ear his whole life. Every time I watched him perform, he had so much confidence on stage and always knew how to entertain the crowd with his jokes. I could tell how much he loved music and performing and it made me want to be just like him. One of our favorite songs to perform together is "As Time Goes By" from the classic movie Casablanca. He and my parents have always believed in me and encouraged me to never give up on my dreams.

I was also influenced by many female artists including Mariah Carey, Martina McBride, Christina Aguilera, LeAnn Rimes, Shania Twain, Kelly Clarkson and Whitney Houston. I love hearing the incredible power and emotion in their voices, along with the empowering song lyrics they sing. There was one Mariah Carey song called "Through The Rain" that I used to listen to, on repeat, whenever I was having a bad day. Even now, it is still one of my favorite songs that I listen to whenever I'm feeling down; it always helps me get back on my feet again. There were times when I just wanted to give up altogether, but I knew I had to keep fighting.

I was in chorus all through middle school and high school, but didn't start taking guitar lessons and writing songs until I was 17. Learning how to play guitar was such a blessing, because now I could write original songs and express my own emotions and experiences through lyrics and melody. I also began taking vocal lessons at the Delco Let There Be Rock School, with the owner Melissa Daley, who is now my vocal coach and manager. Melissa helped me figure out who I was as an artist, and I'm honestly not sure what I would do without her in my life.

When I was on NBC's "The Voice", I shared my personal struggles with academics and bullying. Since then, many have reached out on social media and at shows to tell me how much my story has helped them overcome their own difficulties; that I have given them hope that everything does get better if you just keep fighting. A few have even told me that I was the reason they stood up to their bullies at school. Others have said that I inspired them to keep chasing their dreams and to never give up. There is nothing more rewarding in life then being able to help as many people as you can in this world. I feel that we all need to stick together and help each other out. It makes me so happy knowing that I am able to make a difference in people's lives through my music.

My life could have gone in many different directions, but because of music and my amazing support system, I am where I want to be in life and couldn't be happier. I only hope that I can continue doing what I love and helping others through music.

*Audra Mclaughlin*
*Glenolden, Pennsylvania – U.S.A.*
*www.AudraMclaughlin.com*

## "Music = Emotion"

Like many successful musicians who were fortunate to grow up in a musical household I, too, was exposed to music at an early age. My mom, Ruth Landers, was working full time, and she struggled to support our family, yet managed to save enough money to buy a record player. We would borrow albums from the local library and listen to classical symphonies, jazz greats, rock 'n' roll classics, operettas, Motown, Broadway show tunes, country and gospel music. There were so many different artists and styles that I loved. One artist in particular, Billy Holiday, was very special. For me, her voice was nothing short of raw emotion radiating from the stereo speakers – there was absolutely nothing else like it.

By the time I could talk, I knew I wanted to become a singer. I acted in my first commercial when I was just three years old, and began performing and singing in school plays and local theater groups. While growing up, I also learned how to play the violin, piano and guitar. Throughout my journey, my Mom has been my life-long manager and business partner. Despite not being a musician herself, it was always her encouragement and support that fostered my love for music and led me down this creative path. Although I was only close to my father when I was a very young child, in retrospect, I can appreciate his musical ability. He was always singing and improvising on a variety of instruments, and the five year old little girl in me still remembers his beautiful harmonies.

I have always believed in the synergism of music and education. It was this passion that led me to co-create, with my mom, the award winning public television series, the Huggabug Club, a musical educational series for children. Each of the 47 half hour themed episodes teaches children life lessons through music, song and dance. Part of the extensive research that went into creating the series focused on the power of learning when it is combined with rhythm, rhyme and melodies – songs. I'm very proud to have co-written the more than 200 original songs in the series.

I honestly cannot imagine my life without music. Writing music has always been an emotional outlet for me. Many times, being able to express myself through words and music helped me to understand and cope with life issues and to step back and put things in perspective. It has been an integral part of my career, from the time I wrote my first song at age 11, to my world tours. Music is synonymous with emotions. Music is simply...a part of me.

*Audrey Landers - Star of "Dallas"*
*International Singer/Composer*
*www.AudreyLanders.com*

## *"3 Kinds of People"*

I sometimes get asked how I got into music or why I do it. The answer is simple. All music evokes emotion, it makes you really feel something, which is the very essence of what makes us human. Music can make you happy, it can excite you, it can heal emotional wounds, it can make you sad and can help you recall memories. From an early age, music gave me personal freedom and it has always given me strength and power to take on anything that this world throws at me.

I've always believed that there are 3 kinds of people in this world, those who live in a dream world, those who face reality and those who turn one into the other. Take the things you're good at and be proud of them and share them with the world! Every morning we are reborn into this world...Every day we have the chance to make a new start and live a new life and everyday all kinds of great things are done by ordinary people.

*BARAN – Iranian Pop Singer*
*Los Angeles, California – U.S.A.*
*www.BaranMusique.com*

---

## No matter what you're going through, Music helps make it better.

## "Like A Virgin"

When I was eight years old, I lived with my family in Fresno, California. My two best friends were Steve and Tom Jamison, who lived next door to my grandmother. Steve used to walk around his house singing "Just A Dream", a song by Jimmy Clanton. Steve and Tom were several years older than I was, and I really looked up to them. Steve collected 45's and his collection sparked my interest. Soon, I had records of my own, including "Poor Little Fool" by Ricky Nelson, "Yakety Yak" by The Coasters, "All I Have To Do Is Dream" by The Everly Brothers, "Summertime Blues" by Eddie Cochran, "Come Softly To Me" by The Fleetwoods, "Little Star" by The Elegants and "To Know Him Is To Love Him" by The Teddy Bears. I had a small, felt-covered turn table and I would play these songs over and over. There was something soothing and inspiring in them. It was like a drug. My parents thought there was something wrong with me, because I listened to the records so often. Honestly, it kind of bothered me that none of my friends seemed to care about music as much as I did.

No members of my family were musically inclined or played instruments. While growing up, I actually wanted to be a professional baseball player. Records were my dream world, but it never occurred to me that one could pursue a career in music.

By the time The Beatles came out, my family had moved to Palm Springs, California. I helped form a rock band The Fables and was their lead singer. We played at high school dances, the Palm Springs Youth Center and at private parties. When I was in high school, I began writing poetry and my grandmother bought me a Gibson acoustic guitar that I still have. In my freshman year of college at Bard, in upstate New York, I tried writing music to my poetry for the first time. It worked! Before long, I was writing a song every day and performing them on campus. I suddenly had found my calling.

I trace my success as a songwriter back to those 45's I had as a kid. Of course, I've been inspired by many more artists and types of music. Bob Dylan was a huge influence. I love blues and listened to artists like Robert Johnson, Fred McDowell, Muddy Waters and John Lee Hooker. My musical heroes are too many to mention. The first hit I wrote was "How Do I Make You" by Linda Ronstadt in 1980, a song that was originally inspired by The Knack's "My Sharona".

I still have a large collection of vinyl records and listen to a few records every day. It's part of who I am. Sometimes, it will occur to me that I want to hear an old favorite like Tim Hardin's "Reason To Believe." The music that I love is what inspires me to write songs. I want to contribute, to compete, to express myself.

In 1983, Tom Kelly and I wrote the song, "Like A Virgin". As was our custom, I wrote the lyric first and then got together with Tom to try to put it to music. The lyric was based on events in my personal life. I had extricated myself from a damaging relationship and had met someone new. Tom read the verse lyric:

*I made it through the wilderness*
*Somehow I made it through*
*I didn't know how lost I was*
*Until I found you*
*I was beat, incomplete*
*I'd been had, I was sad and blue*
*But you made me feel*
*Yeah, you made me feel shiny and new*
*Like a virgin...*

His first reaction was to write it as a ballad. This approach didn't work, and eventually we wrote and demoed the song to our satisfaction. Tom sang the demo in falsetto.

In our initial attempts to market "Like A Virgin", we were very disappointed. Several record executives commented, "it's a catchy tune, but no one will ever record a song called, 'Like A Virgin'". Nonetheless, I had great faith in the song and was unwilling to entertain the idea of re-writing it to change the title.

Michael Ostin, a Warner Brothers A&R guy, heard "Like A Virgin" and loved it! He immediately recognized that it would be perfect for their new artist, Madonna. Madonna loved the song and recorded it with producer, Nile Rodgers. It became a #1 hit and is still her signature song. Tom and I went on to write five #1 songs over a 5 year period.

I learned a lot from this experience. I knew in my heart that "Like A Virgin" was a special song, so we opted not to change the composition when many "experts" were advising us to do so. That's when I realized, sometimes it's better to stay with your instincts and follow your own heart. It definitely worked for us!

*Billy Steinberg*
*www.BillySteinberg.com*

---

> # *Music often has the power to know exactly how we're feeling.*

## *"Living Your Life for Happiness"*

My mother had perfect pitch. She could play absolutely anything she heard on records or the radio. I was 4 years old when I started to learn many chords while watching her play, and then slowly began to play piano myself. Not long after that, I heard Ray Charles on the radio for the first time, and that convinced me that music was going to rule my life. I started my first band at the age of 8, and have been in bands ever since. Music has always kept my life feeling wonderful; sharing music gives me an incredible feeling.

After graduating from high school, I went to McNeese University for 5 years to study pre-med. I was still in a band, but for a while, I thought I might become a doctor. For 5 years however, I was a "Surgical Lab Technician" in a hospital owned by 2 doctors. One of the doctors was eventually put in a penitentiary for 20 years, and the other doctor committed suicide. I took that as a sign to quit the medical field and decided that I should stay with Music all of my life.

In 1974, the singers of "Three Dog Night" left the band, but the guitarist, drummer and bass player stayed together to form a new band called "S.S. Fools". A friend of mine from Louisiana that I played in 2 bands with, Jon Smith, joined that band and asked if I would come and sing with them. "Three Dog Night" was my favorite band at the time, so I moved to LA to be their vocalist. We did one album on CBS records, but I left them about a year later. David Paich & Jeff Porcaro (who put "Toto" together) came to about a third of our rehearsals, and when I left "S.S. Fools", I got a call from them asking me to please come and sing with "Toto". That call was the most fantastic thing that ever happened in my life! I sang "Hold The Line" on the 1st album, which so many people loved. On the "Toto IV" cd, we were nominated for 8 Grammy Awards for the song "Rosanna".  We won 6 of those Grammy Awards, which no one had ever done before.  That was truly one of the most amazing nights of my life.

I'm no longer with Toto, but am still touring the world...so many days for about 7 years now.  I love touring.  Doing so many concerts and tours, everywhere in the world, keeps me HAPPIER than I've ever been.  I'm 67 years old now, but touring and concerts make me feel like I'm only 25.  Even though I spend 200 to 250 days a year touring, I absolutely love my life on the road.  Music is the most incredible thing I have in my life and I will never quit touring, ever.

I believe, that anyone who follows their heart into music, will always live a fantastic life.  Even when you are very old, music will always make you feel young.  I recently wrote this song from my years of being in music:

*"Living Your Life For Happiness"*

*You should be living your life,*
*Just to be a friend*
*Try to do nothing wrong*
*Every moment of time you spend*
*There's never a reason, to ignore,*
*Living the life you defend*
*Being the person you want to be,*
*Only brings you happiness*
*Spending your time to make things right,*
*Can bring you more success*

*Keep living your life, for sweet success*
*Just living your life, for Happiness*
*The love of your life,*
*Is what brings you Happiness*
*So keep living your life for Happiness*

*Bobby Kimball*
*www.BobbyKimball.com*

## *"Thanks Mom"*

Strangely enough, she had always wanted me to play more music, my Mom, that is. I had been in a band in college and had also done some solo work after that. We were always very close.

But then I got a business career, and that was followed by having three children in three years. Yeah, life was really busy and I just couldn't fit music into my days.

Then she died.

I sat there, looking at her three grandchildren under the age of 5. They would never know their sweet grandmother and she would never see them grow up. I didn't know how to grieve. There wasn't a lot of time for that either.

That very night it started. Music and lyrics came to me while I was sleeping. It happened over and over again, often waking me up. Original music... I had never written original music before. I started to think I was cracking up. I decided to make a therapy appointment.

Although the therapist gave me validation for my sadness, I left without anything else that was very helpful. A friend of mine suggested I visit a producer friend of his, to try to make sense of the music I was hearing in the middle of the night.

Even though I still cried every morning, that was the beginning of my new life. I now had some place to "put" my emotions. I took the money set aside for therapy and booked studio time instead. That was 22 years ago. My mother's legacy? I love my musical life every single minute of every single day.

Not a day goes by when I don't imagine my mother's smiling face. I'm forever grateful to her for so many things. Even in passing, she is still with me, giving me a reason to wake up every day...to create music!

This story is dedicated to the lasting memory of

Beatrice Rapport Greenfield, always and forever, a dear supporter of the arts!

*Bonnie Warren*
*Plymouth Meeting, PA & Nashville, TN – U.S.A.*
*www.BonnieWarren.com*

## *"Making Mom Happy Again"*

One day I was donating music instruments to an inner city school, in Miami, as part of   our Musical Cares program.  We were donating guitars and keyboards to help get their music program off the ground.  Whenever we visit schools, we like to sit down with some of the students and ask them questions about why they like music and why they think a musical education is important.  This time, we sat down with a young 9 year old boy and asked him why he wanted to learn how to play an instrument.  He told us that his father used to play saxophone and his mother loved hearing him play.  The little boy went on to say that his father died in the war in Afghanistan and his mother had since been very sad.  The sole reason he wanted to learn how to play the saxophone, was to help make his mother happy again.  Even at such a young age, this boy recognized  the immense healing power that music can have.  This experience also reaffirmed my belief that every child should have the opportunity to learn how to play music.

We never know when and where in our lives our musical gifts may be able to help another person.

*Bronsen Bloom*
*Boca Raton, Florida – U.S.A.*
*Founder of Musical Cares*
*www.MusicalCares.com*

## *"The Amazing Avah Grace"*

A courageous baby named Avah suffered unthinkably. After caring health providers, and others helped her survive against all odds, music played a very special role in her ongoing journey. This is some of her story and the tender music miracles we have had the privilege to be a part of.

Music began defining mine and my husband's lives early, in elementary orchestra where we first met. We shared a continued passion for music pursuits and eventually married in 1988, (27 years at this writing). Music became an important facet of our eventually unique and large family.

By the time Avah came into our lives in September, 2011, dozens of foster children of all ages, abilities and challenges, had graced our home. Over a 20-year span of fostering, we had adopted several of these children, in addition to having 3 natural children. We had a full, busy life with a family of eight adult children, and seven younger ones.

Through it all, we deeply valued music's enriching, calming, even *healing* opportunities. So many special needs and fragile children under our wing keenly benefitted from music - educational, therapeutic and otherwise; it was also a boon to our thriving children. Music proved to be a powerful bonding agent and a great source of positivity and joy in our family. We were no strangers to its uplifting powers. Then came Avah.

Avah's story unfolds with a sobering subject: infant abuse, resulting in severe brain injuries known as Shaken Baby Syndrome. She was born healthy and bright, with intelligent, shining eyes. Tragically, all of this, even her emerging, beautiful smile, were all taken from her at just a few weeks old. She endured the worst injuries possible to survive, including several of her tiny ribs sustaining fractures and multiple, severe head injuries. Upon her arrival at the hospital in a coma, she wasn't initially expected to survive.

Weeks later, though not actively fostering anymore, we received the call requesting us to consider doing emergent, short-term care for a fragile child. Hesitantly, I headed to the hospital for the familiar experience of learning about a child's extensive needs. As I understood more of Avah's heart wrenching story, I was deeply moved. Here was a little one, having suffered unimaginably – now blind, deaf and tube-fed.

I soon understood the likely *short-term* request: Avah was not expected to live long. While we could offer such a child quality care, there were seven young reasons at home precluding my bringing such grim circumstances into the family fold. With much mixed feelings, I began talking myself into the exit. Then, something special happened, giving me pause.

Comforting the typical, inconsolable crying of fragile babies takes patience. I didn't expect my swaddled, gentle sways to easily quiet her distraught crying...and they didn't, not at first. Then, she suddenly soothed after I began to hum a quiet, favorite lullaby. I was nicely surprised, but not nearly as much as the hospital staff who had been caring for her. Prior to this unexpected calming response to me and my little tune, her severe, chronic crying had rarely been relieved, except with powerful medications.

Intrigued, and not wishing to *unsettle* her, I opted to spend a little more time with her. Of course, she was constantly disrupted to be poked, prodded or changed. These necessary disturbances upset her, without fail. Time and again, she allowed my soft song to easily sooth her. Curiously, she seemed to have quite a preference for that first melody in particular. With my supportive husband's help back home, my stay extended. I held and rocked and lullabied her back to sleep as needed for several spells, until my arms were intolerably cramped. Her inexplicable affinity for this little lilt, a favorite hymn actually, was poignant and tender to me.

Of course, with all of this, the conflicts in my heart were deepening.

Before deciding anything, I needed to quietly ponder. I needed guidance and strength beyond my capacities and emotional urges. The hospital's cushioned chapel was a reprieve from all the bustle – and offered needed rest for my weary shoulders.

How could I bring home such a fragile baby...possibly, even probably to die? How could I think of putting this on my young children at home? How would we manage her complex care, AND continue taking good care of all the others? Making this decision even more difficult, was the information that with no capable or willing caregivers, Avah would soon be put on a *comfort measures only* hospice plan. If this strong, overcoming little one had any hopes at all, time was of the essence for her to have a seasoned, surrogate mother advocating and caring for her.

As the gravity of all this weighed upon me in the chapel that day, I will always remember the feeling of the burden being lifted from me. I heard in my heart, and head, "You are needed for this... only you can do this...you have been prepared...you will have all you need...have faith".

Time to call my husband, my rock and the devoted father of ALL our other children. He already knew the gist, but what would he say now? Surely, he would remind me of our already full house. There was a long silence after my explanations. Was he frustrated? Overwhelmed? I couldn't have blamed him.

Finally, he just said, "If we are needed to do this...we have been prepared and we will have all we need. It will all work out with faith." My husband's sentiments were uncannily similar to those still echoing within me from the chapel: impressions I had not yet shared with him in detail.

Avah soon came home – to seven children bursting with delight over her, and so many others who were all immediately taken with her. Extended family and friends proved to be generously supportive with our family's complex decision.

Avah fought hard for her life that first year, as she faced several surgeries and serious complications. As her injuries slowly resolved, she was left permanently on a feeding tube, with decimated vision and auditory processing centers, as well as most upper, connective brain tissue – all gone. She would never walk, talk, run or play...never communicate normally. It was thought she would never laugh or sing, or smile again.

We counted every day with our little angel as a blessing – and loved and cared for her with all we had. Her doctors would often just shake their heads with "there is no medical explanation for her still being here". Then, somewhere - in the middle of the many weekly specialist appointments, hospital stays, complex case management, extreme crying bouts, her intensive daily care and many exhausting days and nights - another music miracle happened with Avah.

Determined to maintain as much continuity as possible for our other children, we kept music alive in our home. Many months later, Avah was laying on my lap, just feet away from a young practicing cellist, when the music of Amazing Grace resonated out of our daughter's cello strings and, unexpectedly grabbed Avah's attention. She turned her head toward the sound – a first!

While still unable to see, within moments, she was smiling. Really smiling! Her FIRST real smile! For a long, memorable while, as long as her favorite song vibrated, Avah kept seeking its source, and the beautiful smiles kept coming. This was such an important moment in our lives; a beautiful miracle to be part of. Avah smiled!

The smiles didn't quit and, over time, became genuine

laughter. She continued seeking sounds, especially music. She obviously had begun *hearing* guitar strums, and the piano. Perhaps she could feel the vibrations. She loved it!

Near her first birthday, finally adoptable, we became her forever family, and she became Avah Grace. And there is more. Our family often made music together with various instruments and singing. Avah always brightened to this, and especially to her favorite song. By her second birthday she had begun to engage with the music, in her own special way, by singing along with us! This was more than ever thought possible!

There is no medical explanation for her obvious recognitions, social connections or her musical preferences. Her scans show her left with little more than a brain stem. The miracle of Avah continues to amaze us and baffle her specialists. We don't know what miracles Avah's future holds, musical or otherwise. We do know this: she will soon celebrate another birthday, and lots of loved ones will help her blow out FOUR candles for the bravest little angel, so loved, with all our hearts.

That first little tune, the one she first allowed me to console her with...which coaxed my stay, and quickened essential, deeper connections...you've likely guessed, was her *smile* song, and still her favorite - Amazing Grace.

So, an astounded mother begs the question, for at least the sixteenth time, who are these miracles really for, and who, after all, is blessing who? And so, the power of music continues to define us, brim us with awe, and touch us with exquisite joys.

*Connie Kerbs*
*Clayton, Washington – U.S.A.*
*ConnieKerbs.com*
*www.Facebook.com/AvahsGrace*
*www.ConnieKerbs.com*

## *"Music Saved Me from Myself"*

I thank God for music. Music has been there for me every turn of my life. When I wake up in the morning and when I go to bed at night, I hear music. Music has saved my life over and over again.

There is one particular experience that I don't share lightly. Like many of us, not every chapter of my life has been perfect; I've faced troubles like anyone else. There were issues with family, loss of loved ones and dealing with addictions.

I grew up in an education conscious family. My parents sent me to private school from first grade all the way through graduating high school. I also took private instruction and tutoring while not in school. I then attended Lehigh University in Bethlehem, Pennsylvania. Lehigh is a very competitive private institution where education is taken seriously. It was there at Lehigh University where music saved my life.

Before I get into how music saved me from myself, I have to share a little more of my history. I grew up in the church, and being as such, my morals were significantly fortified. I never smoked or drank or indulged in rebellious behavior in high school. While my classmates were toasting it up with drinks, I was playing card games, having fun with sober friends and writing songs.

When I first went to Lehigh, I was not one to indulge in the social activities of most freshman; parties, drinking, promiscuity or drugs. Unfortunately, during my sophomore year, that began to change. I let my guard down and decided to try drugs and alcohol. It wasn't long after that I became addicted. This lifestyle caught a hold of me and I became a social butterfly. I was hosting parties and at one point was among the inner circle of higher-ups in the drug communities. I never judged the lifestyle, but because of this addiction, other interests became less important to me. I dropped out of school and didn't care that my life had fallen so far down. I didn't let people know what I was going through and was not mature enough to take responsibility for my poor decisions. To me, it seemed that all hope was lost for my own personal journey. I was distanced from a lot of my friends and was running away from my family and God. But, there was something there through it all - my music.

Even though I had dropped out of school, I was still performing with my friends in the music department. I was touring with the choirs, singing with the gospel groups, meeting area musicians and collaborating with them, writing songs, singing, playing piano and recording. This is how music saved me. While every aspect of my life disintegrated to an alarming low, my musical life was thriving! It never let me go when other things had betrayed me, or I, them. Music sang wisdom and guidance into my life. It gave me confidence and a sense of purpose. And, ultimately, having purpose is the most important thing we can have in this life. Music said no to a "drug lifestyle" for me and yes to having me elevate again!

It's because of music that I feel refreshed, purposeful and loved. I just can't say it enough - Thank God for music!

*Derek Anthony Wilson*
*Philadelphia, Pennsylvania – U.S.A.*
*www.TheDerekAnthony.com*

---

> # *Music is a magical time machine that instantly transports us to a special moment in the past.*

---

## A Divine Gift From the Universe"

I am a singer. When people ask, "Oh! What kind of music do you sing?" My answer causes a lot of confusion. This is because, in reality, I am a classical – pop – crossover – Broadway – jazz – singer – songwriter. "Wait. So, you do... everything?" they say. Yes. Sometimes I try to explain it like, "I'm like if Andrea Bocelli and Bette Midler had a baby who hung out with Leonard Cohen". That's what I do. Sort of.

So, Mr. Love Songs is putting together a book about the ways that music changes lives. Music has changed my life - kept me alive - and helped me change other peoples' lives so many times, that it's hard to narrow things down!

I could you tell about the time when I sang operatic arias and Dean Martin and Connie Francis songs at an Italian restaurant. I'd stand on top of a table in the middle of the whole place, and if I hit a high note, the manager would hide in the kitchen and shatter a plate to make it sound like my voice was breaking glass. The whole place would erupt in applause and forget that the kitchen was running behind or the service was slow.

Or once, in India, I went and volunteered at an ashram for lepers. They didn't speak English and I didn't speak Hindi, but I sang for them and they chanted for me and we got along just fine.

Or maybe I can tell you about a friend of mine, a young man with cerebral palsy.

I'm not gonna lie. My 20's were really rough. I got kicked out of Music School because I tried to commit suicide. They told me I could keep my scholarships if I went to rehab. But, after the hospital, I didn't go back. I moved back in with my parents. And during that time, there was a TV show that I watched. It made me laugh and laugh. It was one of the only things I looked forward to during that time of my life. It was called "Just Shoot Me."

Flash forward to years later - that friend of mine with cerebral palsy I just mentioned? I met him because I was singing with another friend, a pianist, at this mall in the Los Angeles suburbs. This young man with CP would come hear us perform and it was months before I learned that his mother was the star of that TV show I loved. One day, after performing at the Westfield Topanga Mall, she approached me and said, "Just so you know, my son listens to your music on YouTube every day. Sometimes 5, 6, 7 times a day!"

I didn't have the courage to tell her then. Like most important things in life, I just wait 'til I'm onstage and then make a joke about it - about how amazing is it that SHE HERSELF gave ME so much joy at a time when very little made me happy. Now, it was an honor for me to give back to her son.

I almost didn't make it in life. And this? This was one of the most divine gifts from the universe: a connect the dot from her heart to my heart to her son's heart through music.

How wondrous these unseen events, this blue orb in the heavens spinning with so many delights! If only we could stay a little bit longer than we think we should, just to see the light dazzle in another's eyes, the song linger in all our ears and hearts. For if I had done the deed and I had not lived, I would never receive THIS moment, this "proof" that it was all for some very important reason that each of us was put here on earth.

*Erin Carere*
*Los Angeles, California – U.S.A.*
*www.WorldOfErin.com*

## "Standing on the Shoulders"

Everyone has their reasons why they got into music. Before I even began playing guitar at age 12, I was motivated by Elvis Presley and Buddy Holly. I was only 6 when Buddy Holly died, but some of the mythology behind the man, as well as who he was, made a big impact on me. He was easily my first real inspiration as a singer, songwriter and performer. The Beatles hit when I was 11, and with that, I clearly saw the future of being able to write, sing and play my own songs. I'd be lying if I didn't say I also saw it as a way to meet girls. I was a drummer at first, then moved to guitar and started writing songs. Later, when I began writing music for film and TV, the nature of how I was recording led me to the piano and I've since become a reasonably good keyboardist.

I know that today there's a real problem with public schools not funding music programs. As a kid, we had band and orchestra from elementary school through high school. I was definitely helped by these programs and believe music should always be an option for children and young adults. The more chances talented kids have to be among others who are like-minded, and to be mentored by a good teacher, the more valuable their learning experiences will be. No matter what you're playing, it's a great opportunity as a child to start understanding the power of playing with others. I felt the same joy at 14 years old when I started my own band...it was like a team.

I grew up in Long Island...about 45 minutes from Manhattan. At that time, it was unheard of in our community for someone to want to become a professional musician. When my parents would tell their friends that I was leaving high school at 16 to make a life as a musician, they would all say "we're so sorry", as if I was terminally ill. In that day and age, it would have sounded better if I had gone off to join the circus. After leaving, I soon found some opportunities in Toronto to perform my own songs, as well as produce other people. I was like a scientist when it came to making records and found creating music in the studio spellbinding. When I accidentally fell into producing and arranging at the young age of 19, I felt like I had found a calling. It wasn't a calling to perform, but one to help make other people sound the best they could be by being the director of the recording.

My older brother Larry, who is still my best friend, was the Mollin son to go to college and was a tremendous support for me during this time. While away at university, his creative mind opened up and he began to better understand me. For my entire career, he has been my constant support and my first real help in turning my music into something professional. My mother, now turning 97 and still sharp as a tack, was also very supportive. She always said "If that's what you want, I believe in you". My dad was hopeful, but just not as involved, as he worked tirelessly. By 1985, I had become a film and TV series composer (don't ask...I fell into it) and I was slammed with work as I learned while I earned. My dad was a hard working provider for our family, and when he passed away in 1989 at the age of 76, I had a situation that I hope honored him. He never wanted me to jeopardize a job for anything, but during this tragedy, I was in the middle of a strict deadline, composing scores for a TV series. I had to take time off to fly down to Florida, be there with my family for funeral arrangements and then fly back with the casket to New York for his burial. Altogether, I lost 4 days, but still managed to make my deadline and didn't cause stress with the producers and Paramount Television. Composing for film/TV is very much a craft. I definitely found myself lost in sadness while composing that week, so I'm sure the sentiment was reflected in that episode. I did feel it was OK: It was what my dad taught by example: Get the job done and don't lose the job.

In addition to composing for film and TV, I've also been blessed to have worked with some of the greatest songwriters of our time. With Jimmy Webb, in particular, I've been producing and acting as his musical director since I was 22 years old. Jimmy is considered to be America's greatest songwriter, and I agree. Now, 40 years working with Jimmy, he is still my number one client. On many levels, he's truly part of my family and one of my closest friends. His album, "Ten Easy Pieces", is one of the defining projects of both of our lives and probably the greatest experience where I feel I caught lightning in a bottle. The circumstances at the time were very stressful, but the end result was amazing and the experience changed Jimmy's life.

Through it all, I have an immense gratitude for this wonderful musical life I've lived. I worked very hard and have had such an incredible run, but please know that I am blessed to have the gifts to do what I do.

To all the young people who want to make a musical life for themselves: Please promise me that you'll listen to all the greats in musical history. We all become better artists and songwriters when we stand on the shoulders of those who came before us. Whether you are writing instrumentals or songs, it all starts with the composition. The worst thing you can do, is to not believe that the song is the first and most important thing you start with. If you're going to be a songwriter or composer, please make it so your work will stand the test of time. Try to write something that will be considered a major work, as opposed to a throw-away. Lead, don't follow: You accomplish this by challenging yourself and working hard to be the best you can be. If tomorrow's musicians can find the time to do that, if they can find friends in school to make music together, to spend time getting better and not wasting valuable music writing and playing time on the internet and on social media, then I think we'll be okay.

Kids: Work hard and dedicate your attention and time to your music.

*Fred Mollin*
*Nashville, Tennessee – U.S.A.*
*TV/Film Composer & Record Producer*
*www.FredMollin.com*

## *"The Path of a Professional Musician"*

After a childhood that included being abandoned by my father and abused by my stepfather, I managed to overcome long odds of ever making anything of myself to eventually become a professional musician. To try and make a very long story short, it will have to begin with my parents break up when I was around six years of age. Prior to their divorce, I remember well the constant yelling between my mom and dad all through the long nights. These loud arguments left a scar that may never completely heal. Devastated by the absence of my father, I fell into a pitch black bottomless pit, of which I sometimes still struggle to crawl out of.

Being the only boy out of three children, I must have had an enormous love for my father to have missed him so much when he suddenly left. I still have fond memories of my dad teaching me to play baseball and how he would take the family to our favorite swimming hole in Little Reed Island Creek. Most of our Sundays after church were spent together at my cousin's house, listening to them sing and play their guitars, mandolins and banjos. It seems that every one of my cousins, aunts and uncles played an instrument and sang songs. They would spend hours singing hymns and bluegrass, as I listened and soaked it all up.

After my dad left, it was a very dark and ugly year of moving from place to place, by train, all the way to Louisiana and then back to Virginia. We finally settled in a small Southwestern Virginia town called Dublin. My mom, two sisters, and myself, along with a new step father set up house in this little town. At the beginning of my new life in Dublin, I was happy. Being dragged halfway across the country and back had not worked well for me, but suddenly I found myself in a place that felt good for a change. By the time I was eight or nine years old, I was playing guitar and singing and well on my way to being the best in my little town; something I had vowed to myself that I would one day be. I found friends that I could share my music with and taught a few to play music with me.

One bright spot while growing up was my 5th grade teacher Mrs. Jervey, who without realizing it, played a huge role in my early childhood. She was the first person to ever take an interest in my musical talent, and was also the first to ask me to play in front of an audience. That was 1968 when I was just 10 years old. With her encouragement, I took to the stage like a pro. She gave me confidence and opened a door to the music world that would never close. That was eons ago and I'm still making music to this day. Had it not been for Mrs. Jervey, who knows what path I might have chosen. While she was helping to build my confidence, our home life was slowly falling apart. My step father had begun abusing my mother and was showing signs that he didn't want mom's children, he only wanted her. When I was still a teen a decision was made and I was subsequently forced out of my home. Suddenly, I was living on the street or at anyone's home that would let me stay for a while. Faced with a decision that no child should ever have to make, I quit school to make money and survive. The many years of physical and verbal abuse from my step father scarred me deeply, but it also gave me a strong will to survive and succeed at the only thing I knew how to do, play music!

This was the 70's, and my journey started out shaky at best. Drugs helped provide an escape from a world that spun out of control. It felt like the world that left me empty, cold and alone, so I clung onto the one thing I knew best: music. With my guitar on my shoulder, I hit the road, never to look back or regret anything that I would face in the following years.

I am now in my fifties and my music career has been an interesting journey, to say the least. Music has taken me to places that most people only dream of going. I have known, performed and recorded with some of the most talented people on the planet. I've had the opportunity to see the sunrise in several different countries. I've gazed upon the volcanoes of the western United States and driven practically every inch of the eastern seaboard. Having lived in several major cities, I've learned about the many different cultures that make up our nation. My life experiences through the avenues of music are truly my most cherished memories. It has not always been financially rewarding and is sometimes a very bumpy ride. However I am blessed beyond measure with the talents bestowed upon me, and the choices I made so long ago to walk the path of a professional musician.

One last note about music and connecting with people: When Mrs. Jervey passed away in 2012, I was saddened and disappointed in myself for never taking the time to let her know how much I appreciated what she did for me. I know that she would have been very proud. After being asked to share my story, I began thinking that she must have surviving family members, so I set out to find them. I have recently connected to her youngest son Tom who was really moved by what I had to say in my story. Tom told me that he knew she had an impact on a lot of people, but this was the first time he had ever seen anyone write about it. Tom's dad was equally moved and sent me a letter stating that he was going to add the story to her memorial. The moral of this is, don't be afraid or hesitate to let someone know how much you appreciated having them in your life. None of us will live forever. Sharing music, stories and everything that helps make us human, truly serves to make our voyage on earth just a little bit brighter.

*Gary Alexander*
*Nashville, Tennessee – U.S.A.*
*www.GaryAlexanderMusic.com*

---

## No one ever regrets being a musician, but many regret having never played.

---

### *"Saved by the Guitar"*

When I was 10 years old, I remember waking up one morning to the sounds of Baker Street by the Gerry Rafferty Band. My siblings and I had fallen asleep with the clock radio on and the dimly lit 3:33 was the first thing my eyes could make out. We were staying the night in an unused room at the Holiday Inn where my Dad worked. For us, this was just another chapter in our tumultuous childhood. As I lay there motionless, I could feel the music drifting into my ears and easing into my soul. It was mysterious and familiar at the same time, and I felt an urging to sing. The sounds of the guitar and saxophone lifted me up, and I knew then I wanted to be able to make that sound. I wanted to do whatever they were doing because of the way it made me feel: Safe. Loved. Empowered. I didn't have the words to describe it then.

Playing the guitar saved my life. I grew up in a broken home full of violence, drugs, and creepy people. I left home at 11, then again at 16. Eventually, I ended up in front of a judge who said "I'm sending you to prison". A miracle and some money got me house arrest instead. The conditions: stay out of any and all trouble with the police. I didn't think I could do it. I considered leaving the country. In a serendipitous moment, my sister Jennifer, who I had not seen in over a year, dropped off an electric guitar on my front porch. These were my first strums on an electric guitar through an amp, and the experience was identical to what I felt at 10 years old. Incredible bliss! I vowed to stay out of trouble and to learn how to play this amazing instrument.

It wasn't long before I was in a band playing shows and having great fun playing "rock star". Unfortunately, I then found out my band mates were arrested for robbing banks. The band was done, my dream crushed, and I began searching for more in life. I spent time learning wilderness survival. I was intrigued by the traditional vision quest of the Native Americans, so I embarked on my own 96 hour quest in the wilderness...alone. No food. No pen, paper, knife, phone or people. Just me and the wild things. I was driven to find a Vision for my life. Willing to bear the pain. It was scary at night. Things moved about. My stomach burned with hunger. I cried. I screamed. I slept. I dreamed. Four days later I walked out of the woods a different man. My Vision was clear: to use mentoring and music to help change lives.

My Vision led me to Washington DC, where I started teaching guitar. I found enjoyment creating a specialized guitar method for adults. But violence continued to follow me. One afternoon, my Dad and I were violently attacked by a gang of young kids, in broad daylight. Then, another time, 2 teenagers held me at gunpoint. I realized that someone needed to teach these kids a lesson...a guitar lesson! My Vision became clearer. I began to volunteer teaching at-risk youth how to play guitar. In many cases, the kids got to keep their guitars. They earned them. I have also put many of these kids on stages to perform, when they felt comfortable. I'm blessed to have many supporters for my mission including Dweezil Zappa, who has helped fund programs, share what I do with others, and even brought one young man on stage to perform with him. My Grand Vision is to bring the entire world together in a unified Global Jam 4 Peace. Coming soon so stay tuned!

*Gregg Hammond ~ "Music is My Magic Wand"*
*Washington, D.C. – U.S.A.*
*www.dcguitarlessons.com*
*www.reverbnation.com/gregghammond*

## "The Decision Chair"

Not everyone can point to the precise moment when the decision was made to pursue a career. Not only am I able to do that, but I can also identify the exact chair in which I was sitting when I made the decision to become a college choral conductor.

I don't actually recall the exact date, but it was either a Saturday or Sunday, (June 6 or 7) 1970, at the end of my junior year as a very mediocre accounting major at Loyola University. It may, or may not, have actually been Paul Salamunovich's birthday, but it was the day of the annual end-of-the-year party at the Salamunovich's house. The members of Men's Chorus and Mount Singers had pooled their money to buy Paul a state-of-the-art Wenger conductor's chair. I was asked, as president of Men's Chorus, to make the presentation. We hauled the chair up onto the roof of the shed behind his house at the end of the driveway. I brought along my tux, which I put on, but I still wore the volleyball shoes I had been wearing all day to play in the driveway. We agreed to sing the opening chant from Hermann Schroeder's Te Deum, which we had performed several times that semester. So, I climbed up on that roof in my tux and volleyball shoes with a Lum's schooner of beer in my left hand. I had never conducted anything in my life, but I sat on the chair and mimicked the way I had seen Paul conduct thousands of times. Then three things happened: 80 members of the chorus standing in the driveway began following me and singing; I made the decision in that instant to become a college choral conductor while thinking "What a cool way to make a living!"; and Paul ran by me below and threw a cup of beer at me. I will say that his recollection of this last detail differs from mine, and perhaps we'll need someone else to help us sort out our memories.

Over the next 23 years, I went through the process of getting my music degrees and teaching certification, and working my way up through years of teaching junior and senior high school, until I landed my first college choral music position in 1993. When I was visiting Paul and his wife Dottie at their home in January 2008, I mentioned that June day in 1970. Paul remembered it very clearly, and said that the chair was now stored in that same shed upon which I sat that day. Paul had continued to use the chair at Loyola for another twenty years, until he left in 1991 to become the director of the Los Angeles Master Chorale. After that, he continued to use it for another ten years at the Los Angeles Music Center.

In April 2009, the host for the 2010 Pennsylvania Collegiate Choral Association Festival had to back out and I was asked to step in and host it at Clarion University. I immediately got on the phone and asked Paul if he would be our guest conductor, and just as quickly, he accepted.

So, in February 2010, he spent five days in Clarion where we got to reconnect and share our passion for choral music. On the drive back to the airport on Sunday, Dottie, who was riding in the back seat with my wife Cyndi, made a comment about wanting to downsize and distribute some of the things in their house and in storage to their children. I quickly chimed in with, "You know, that chair has some sentimental value to me." At that point, Paul turned around and stated, "Dottie, the chair's Hank's!" Four months later, on Father's Day, I called Paul to say hello. Dottie answered the phone and we chatted for a while. Then she called to Paul, "Hank's on the phone." His first words to me were, "Hank, the chair's yours. Come and get it."

My brother Chris drives trucks for the movie studios and his occasional trips to Universal Studios take him close to Paul's home in North Hollywood. One day, in August 2010, I came home and found a large box on my porch containing the very conductor's chair on which I sat 40 years earlier when I made the decision to become a college choral conductor. I have been fortunate to have directed choral music at the college level for over twenty years now. After receiving the chair, I initially used it just as it had arrived - scratched, dirty, the upholstery worn and torn. After one semester I cleaned and painted it and had it reupholstered. Currently it sits in a rehearsal hall at Kutztown University of Pennsylvania where I am Director of Choral Studies. I think of Paul every time I look at it and sit in it and am inspired by the legacy it represents. Professionally, it is my most prized and treasured possession.

*Dr. Hank Alviani*
*Clarion, Pennsylvania – U.S.A.*
*Director of Choral Studies*
*Kutztown University of Pennsylvania*

## *"Together for Just One Night"*

I've always been a believer in giving back, so in 2003, I started my non-profit organization called the Jana's Kids Foundation. This organization exists as a way to address issues with Native youth and to encourage them to succeed in life. Being of Native American heritage myself, I understood the struggles and adversities that many of them go through. I wanted to help inspire the Native youth through my music and by sharing my own experiences with them. Since 2006, our foundation has also awarded scholarships to Native youth for academic, artistic and athletic achievement. Through all my experiences with the Jana Kids Foundation, I knew that I could make a positive change in another human being's life through music. What I didn't realize was how much I would, one day, be impacted by sharing my music with others.

A few years ago, I was asked to sing for terminally ill children at the Ronald McDonald house in New York. I readily agreed to do this, but honestly, I had trepidation from the moment they asked me. I knew the unforeseeable sadness that would overcome me once I saw the children's faces. I really admire the workers, volunteers, parents and anyone involved in helping terminally ill children on an ongoing basis. To me, I knew it would feel so heartbreaking to see these children and know they only have a short time remaining on this earth. To be strong is an understatement for the adults, but what I discovered was that the real strength comes from the kids themselves. As I entered the room where I was about to sing, I was truly surprised to see the beaming smiles on the children's faces, their laughter and chatter filling the space.

Music has long been lauded as therapy for the sick, both physically and mentally. It heals in so many ways, but it's not just for those on the receiving end; it's very often just as healing for the giver too. Singing my music has always been therapeutic for me. On that particular night, thankfully, it kept me together before falling apart. There were numerous times I just wanted to break down and cry. But I asked myself, who am I to feel sorry for them? Seeing their bright smiles looking back at me as I sang was an irreplaceable joy for me. They sang along and danced with me, as if absolutely nothing was wrong. One very young girl in particular, her hair completely gone from the chemo, had a giggle so adorable you just wanted to squeeze her cute little cheeks. She immediately seemed to latch on to me and connect to my music. I held her hand and together we danced with such excitement. Through her smiles, you never would have guessed the pains she had endured in her few short years of life. Though I was supposed to be the one offering these children momentary happiness through music, they were the ones who ultimately gave me hope. They not only changed my life in that moment, but I carry it with me still to this day. Sadly, shortly after I performed at the Ronald McDonald House, the little girl with the adorable little giggle passed away. The strength and fearlessness of this child was greater than even the strongest, healthiest person in the world. Music brought us together for just one night, but I will forever be inspired to never give up because of it.

*Jana Mashonee*
*New York, New York – U.S.A.*
*www.JanaMashonee.com*

# One night of music may inspire a lifetime of memories.

## *"I Don't Believe in Plan B"*

I have had the good fortune and privilege to live my entire adult life working in music... sometimes as a singer, sometimes as a songwriter and for the last couple of decades as a Film & TV composer.

Although, like any artist, many components and 'synchronicities' (some call it luck) occurred along the way of my 40+ years music career, the foundation for my travels lies very simply with my parents support. Although I was fortunate to receive any lessons I asked for as a young boy (piano lessons at age eight for a couple of years, guitar lessons, accordion, trumpet), I really didn't settle into any of them until my mid-teens when I discovered a love (and a bit of a knack) for composing, which led me back to piano.

My parents, although curious as to why I had some trouble sticking with a particular instrument, never wavered in their support. My mother was a very musical person. Although she did not pursue a music career, she was a singer, dancer and someone who had an uncanny ability to remember the lyrics and most melodies from almost the entire American Standard songbook... from the 1920's through the 1960's! There was practically nothing that could be said in our home that she didn't turn into a song. That certainly influenced me as a songwriter/composer. My father (who was not as musically inclined) was possibly the best example of support. I say this, because he really didn't like the idea of me going into music as a profession. He did not see it as viable or as a way for me to support myself or a family. Even though he expressed those concerns, he never wavered in his support once I made my choice. A very loving act.

These things influenced my own parenting. Although I would have supported any choice my kids made for their life/professions/job, two out of three of them are wonderful singer/songwriter/musicians with two albums released (The Belle Brigade), and the third is a gifted ballet dancer, who at 15, has just been accepted to the Royal Ballet of London summer conservatory.

I guess my point is this: as parents, the biggest gift you can give to your offspring is your support of their dreams and hopes, whether it be music or anything else. I was never told to consider a Plan B. I don't believe in Plan B. At some point, Plan B will start to manifest and interfere with Plan A, if you make too much space for it. If your parents were not, or are not, around to support your Plan A, go for it anyway with all your might. The worst that happens is that Plan B will reveal itself later. Follow your musical dream, or any dream...even if it just turns out to be a hobby in the end.

*Jay Gruska*
*Composer/Songwriter/Producer*
*www.JayGruska.com*

## "Connecting from the Heart"

Music has gotten me through every difficult part of my life. It was always the best way for me to express my true emotions; it was my best friend, my diary. Writing songs is such a cathartic experience and I always found that, whatever was bothering me consciously or unconsciously, would appear through the experience of pouring my thoughts out in music and lyrics.

As a child, I watched both of my parents write, play and perform music, so I knew it was the path that I wanted to take for as long as I can remember. It is often said "If you truly love what you do, you will never work a day in your life", and even as a little girl, I believed this. Music keeps you young, inspired, adventurous and blissful. Too many of us forget to take time out of our busy schedule to just live and do what makes us happy. Music often helps us to remember what that's all about.

I played violin in elementary and middle school and later switched to chorus in high school. I also began taking piano lessons when I was about ten and taught myself the guitar and drums after that. Taking music classes throughout school gave me a stage to practice on. It gave me somewhere to learn and play with like-minded people with a common ground. It also gave me an escape from the stressors of the rest of the school day. I am a huge advocate for keeping music programs in our education system. Music is so powerful and kids today really need something inspiring and freeing to help them navigate through adolescence.

My most touching musical moment that I will remember for the rest of my life was performing a song called "Pretty", while on tour in Colorado. I had written the song shortly before we left and I wasn't sure how people, particularly women, would react to it. When I wrote it, I felt a very special connection with the song, as it really came from my heart and the struggles I dealt with growing up as a young woman learning to love myself, imperfections and all.

We were playing an acoustic set to a large and boisterous crowd and I was particularly nervous about trying out such a slow intimate song in that setting. I went with my gut, said a few words to describe what the song was about and began to play. Halfway through the first verse, I heard sobbing. I looked to my left to see a young woman with tears streaming down her face. Very quickly, my own eyes began to tear up. Despite spending our lives living so far apart and growing up in different circumstances, we discovered we were still the same. Something as powerful as a message through music brought two strangers together as sisters; feeling the same feelings and fighting the same battle...to accept ourselves as we are. It was at that moment that I realized something amazing: not only had this beautiful woman in front of me connected with my story, but I had also touched hearts beyond my wildest dreams, as every woman in the room could be seen gracefully acknowledging our bond as they touched up their makeup.

After the song was over, I went to the young woman who truly inspired me and hugged her tight. I learned a really significant lesson that day that I will carry with me forever: The influence of words and music is so far beyond anything else in this world. Those of us that have the gift are privileged to share it with others. We should always remember, that by sharing our music, we really can make a difference in people's lives.

*Jessica Lynn*
*Westchester, New York – U.S.A.*
*www.JessicaLynnMusic.org*

## *"Never Believe Them"*

When I was 12 years old, music helped me get through my Grandmother's sickness and passing. Each day after school, I would visit and help take care of her during her struggles with cancer. Music always helped to comfort her and became a strong connection we shared. She would always ask me to sing her a song, and before she died, I wrote a special song to sing to her. Since that time, I have used music to help relieve stress whenever difficulties come up in my life. Music has shaped my mind to always be open, and enabled me to encourage others to venture out of their comfort zone. Music helps us all connect with other people and spread messages of hope and inspiration to others in need.

To all the other creative people out there, I say to you: "Never believe them when they say you're not good enough. The music you have in your heart may someday change someone's life. If you don't share your music, then we'll never know."

*JKELL*
*Chesapeake, Virginia – U.S.A.*
*www.JKellsWorld.com*

## *"If You Don't Dream Big, Why Dream at All"*

Like many musicians before me, I'm just a small town boy with big dreams of helping to change the world. I've always had a passion for writing and would often sit on a hay stack in front of the dairy cattle to write out song lyrics. Eventually, I started setting my words to melodies and began singing these songs for audiences, wherever I could. I've always felt that songs are like a 3 minute storybook, filled with all the rhythm and harmony that speak to the heart. Music is also a healer, it's our greatest medicine and is the only language that can be understood anywhere on this planet of ours. To me, music is much more than just a song played on the radio, in a club or at a rehearsal. Music is passion and feeling; it can ease the pain of the broken hearted, spark the fire to a new love and keep peace between a world in chaos.

My goal is to spread the message of sharing and compassion, not only through music, but in my actions every day. My Grandpa always preached to me "do not do something big in life for just yourself, always stay kind and involve others in your success, especially those who are in need". With his advice always in my mind, I strive to touch one life at a time through my passion for music and helping others.

This summer, we hope to launch the very first "Saving Soldiers" tour that will visit many cities in the U.S. I'm a Navy veteran myself. I know, first hand, that the needs of our soldiers are often not being met, especially when they return home. We want to do anything we can to help them in their adjustment back to life in the U.S.A. It's a big, but, also, very important mission and as I always say "If you don't dream big, then why dream at all"!"

*Joey James*
*Salem, Oregon – U.S.A.*
*www.JoeyJamesBand.com*

## "It's Not All Unicorns and Rainbows"

For many of my teenage years, music was all I had. I would have a rough day at school and just couldn't wait until the bell would ring and I'd soon be back home listening to cassettes of my favorite bands. I was going through a lot at the ages of 13-16; lots of family problems and problems I had with myself. Music helped to make sense of all of it, just by listening to it. Then, I started playing along with those same songs and albums with my guitars and piano. Some of my favorites growing up were Jackson Browne, The Allman Brothers Band, Guns N' Roses, Van Morrison, Counting Crows, Bob Dylan and The Beatles.

My father was also a big influence on me and my music while growing up. He had a phenomenal taste in music and an amazing record collection with only the best stuff. He sat me down on many nights when I was 10, 11, 12 years old and had me listen to Van Morrison or Chuck Berry or the Grateful Dead. It opened my eyes to what was out there, beyond what my friends in middle or high school were listening to. Back then, he would sing in "doo-wop" groups in north-eastern New Jersey, right around when he was my age now. He also bought me my first acoustic guitar, my first electric guitar and my first piano. Whenever I needed it most, he pushed me just enough.

When my father bought me my first Martin acoustic guitar, he set up lessons with a professional outside of school. I was actually doing pretty well on the guitar at that point, but professional lessons really helped me to understand both the physical and philosophical aspects of an instrument. Guitar is not the easiest instrument to play. I'm not joking when I say it takes practice every day to learn it competently. Never, ever give up.

Along the way, I've been touched, so many times, by how music has affected people around me. It comes up at almost every show. Someone comes up and says "hey, this song really reminds me of my mom and she passed away a few years ago, can you play it?" I say "I can", and I do. Sometimes they cry, sometimes everyone claps and the people want to buy me shots or beers at the bar. It's all good. Any kind of joy I can bring to someone through music is good for me. That's why I do it. One time, this girl told me she had my album playing on her iPod while she was running early in the morning. She came upon a long hill, aching, about to pass out, trying her best. When she finally reached the top, she saw the sun. At that moment, my song "Before It Goes Out" was playing on her iPod; she said she broke down crying, because of how beautiful the horizon looked, early on a summer morning and how she kept pushing herself to get healthier. She was feeling better about herself every day and music was a part of that.

Music has always been there for me and for that, I'm always thankful. It's given me the opportunity to travel around the country and I wouldn't trade it for anything. That's not to say there aren't some occasions that are more difficult; it's not all Unicorns and Rainbows, it's somewhere in the middle. But, if you believe in your sound and know that it's good enough, the sky is the limit. You just have to keep on pushing, playing and doing what you love to do!

*Jordan White*
*Lehigh Valley, Pennsylvania – U.S.A.*
*www.JordanWhiteMusic.com*

## "Maybe It's You"

As a child growing up in Waterville, Maine I was in a difficult family situation. To cope, I turned to food, eating my troubles and anxieties away until by the age of twelve I was nearly 200 pounds. The one good thing I had going in my life was that my mother had seen to it that I had piano lessons. It wasn't long before I realized that I loved to sing and play music.

I was bullied mercilessly in junior high school - especially in the cafeteria. I eventually started spending my lunch time in the music room, which was always empty at that time of the day. I began bringing my popular music books to school with me so I could practice. One day, I was sitting at the piano belting out Carly Simon's "The Right Thing to Do" when someone began clapping. I turned, in horror, to see our choral director, Mr. Monteith, standing in the doorway. He said, "I didn't know you could sing like that! I want you to do a solo in the spring concert!" I was so embarrassed and afraid of what others would say that I declined. He insisted, however, and that afternoon he announced it to the rest of the chorus. After class, I was pinned against the wall in the hallway by a group of girls who informed me that no one wanted to hear me sing. I was commanded to tell Mr. Monteith that I would not perform the solo. I went home crying and the next day, I told Mr. Monteith that I didn't want to do it. When he asked me why, I told him what had happened. That afternoon, he read the group the riot act, and told them in no uncertain terms that I was doing a solo and that was final.

The day of the concert came...and when I came forward to take the microphone, I was shaking uncontrollably. I could see the kids in the audience whispering and hear their snickering. Mr. Monteith played the piano intro of "Maybe it's You," a song by my favorite group, The Carpenters, and I began to sing. Immediately the snickering stopped. I sang the whole song and finished to what to me sounded like thunderous applause. Then, I sang Michael Jackson's "Ben" and got the same reaction.

After the concert, I was approached by a group of girls who congratulated me and said things like, "You really showed 'em, Judy!". These were girls who had been afraid to talk to me before, lest they be targeted as well. Now, they were bold enough to step forward and be my friend. From that day on, my life at school changed. I became known as the girl who could sing, and later, the girl who could write songs. During our senior year of high school, I was asked to write our class song and have since gone on to study music in college and had a wonderful career as an independent artist. I've never stopped making music, and at the ripe old age of 51, I was nominated for a Grammy Award for Best Children's Album....all because of what Mr. Monteith did for me that day. I will be forever grateful for how he and music changed my life.

*Judy Pancoast*
*Manchester, New Hampshire – U.S.A.*
*www.JudyPancoast.com*

## "Don't Give Up!"

I am a singer, songwriter, and actress and recently completed my debut album including the single "Don't Give Up". This song is very dear to me, because it sends out a message to "believe in yourself" and to know that "we are all special" in our own unique way!

I was bullied in middle school, so I know firsthand how hard it can be to live with that every day. I also have a brother with special needs, and he often goes through difficult times with people who are not aware of his situation. I hope my story encourages others who may be dealing with the same things I have, or some of the things I see happen with my brother.

When I was in middle school, I didn't really fit in with all the other students. I wasn't wearing name brand clothes and hardly wore any make up. As a result, I had only a few friends and mostly kept to myself. I was, however, always put in the middle of drama...starting with the first day of school. I was told about an awful rumor that was spreading like wildfire around the school about me. The person spreading this rumor was, I thought, my friend. Things just grew from there and I was made fun of, teased and excluded. I was into singing, theatre and dancing and I guess to them this wasn't "cool". I was put down by my peers and even by some of my instructors. When I was in show choirs and theatre camp, they would say things like "you aren't good enough for a solo or major role". I was always in the background, given minor roles and usually placed in the ensemble.

After a while, I began to question myself..."Was I that bad at what I love to do?" My self-esteem was crushed! My parents started to see that I was pulling back from any type of social interaction. They encouraged me to explain to them exactly what was bothering me. Finally, I told them everything. They immediately pulled me out of the public school I was attending and transferred me to a local private school to complete my middle school education. After that, I was enrolled in home-school for my high school years. Being home-schooled allowed me to fully pursue my career in singing and acting. I auditioned for another theatre program and landed a lead role! I started to sing at any and all coffee houses and open mic nights that I could find. This is where I finally began to realize that I had what it takes to make something of myself...doing what I love.

In addition to the message of "believing in yourself", I also feel very strongly about those who have served our country. My grandfather is a veteran and served in the U.S. Army during the Vietnam War. Inspired by his stories, I co-wrote another song on my album entitled, "Something to Stand For" with Nashville songwriter Chuck Thomas. This song is dedicated to ALL who have served, or are currently serving in our military. It was written to Honor them and Thank them for their service and for our freedom. Last summer, I was performing at a festival and dedicated it to all who serve in our military...past & present. As I began, a man walked up to the front of the crowd. As he listened intently to every word I was singing, he began to cry. During the song, I walked up and began singing to him, and gave him a hug. I had to hold back a few tears myself so I could finish my song. After the show, he came up to thank me, saying that he was a veteran, and that my song had really touched his heart. It was at that moment that I realized and saw firsthand that telling a story through music can help people and bring us all closer together. It's a moment I will never forget.

I have been truly blessed, and I thank God every day for all He has given me! I understand what it is like to be "left out" and to be "made fun of" by your peers. It Hurts! But, I have learned to overcome and rise above it! I learned to do what makes ME happy and pursue my dreams, and to never let ANYONE tell me that "I'm not good enough". Being able to express my feelings through my music has made a real difference in my life, and for that I am forever grateful. Because of the negative experiences I've had early in life, I have decided to write inspirational songs with messages to help encourage people. Writing and performing has truly helped me "move on" with my life and my career, and I can only hope that I can inspire others to do the same.     Always remember to never let anyone bring you down...follow your own heart and "Don't Give Up!" God Bless.

*Kelsey Coan*
*Mount Ephraim, New Jersey – U.S.A.*
*www.KelseyCoanMusic.com*

## *"Birth of an Artist"*

Growing up in a house full of music, instruments, and frequent trips to the theatre to watch his sister and brother sing, my son Joseph comes to music honestly. Like many kids, his response to music is obvious and immediate. Never shy to break out the dance moves or air guitar to express his approval. So, it was no surprise that Joseph quickly gravitated toward the variety of musical instruments that lay around the house  Whether it was sitting at the piano, strumming a guitar or drumming with whatever he could get his hands on, Joseph made music.

My son Joseph has Cerebral Palsy (CP). This is something I always leave out when I think of or talk about him. It doesn't define him. It doesn't define anyone. It comes with assumptions and expectations that are often inaccurate and unfair; assumptions that make parents, like me, cringe in discomfort and frustration.

Joseph is also non-verbal (so far). Something I also leave out. I have the luxury of leaving this one out, because Joseph has a voice – a computer generated voice that he is very capable of using and sharing. Although his hands are one of the parts of his body most affected by his palsy, Joseph has sufficient control to operate his computers touch screen in order to communicate. With every touch of the screen he becomes more accurate and efficient. His computer, as a result, serves the dual purpose of also providing a form of physical therapy for Joseph's arms, hands and fine motor skills (but don't tell him that).

And, it is this technology that has become the greatest source of liberation for our son. Liberating his ideas which are as uncensored, funny and sometimes hurtful, deep and poetic as any child's.

This is where the story begins. In finding his voice, Joseph also found opportunity, friendship and music. And, at the heart of it all, were the teachers and Communication Professionals that recognized Joseph's distinctive ability to turn a phrase, then light up everyone around him and quickly take over a room.

Enter Paul Alcamo, Joseph's SK teacher at Holland Bloorview School Authority and close friend. They are two pals...constantly teasing, testing, and yes, teaching each other. For my son and all of his students, Paul is a constant source of inspiration, creativity, motivation and possibilities; a teacher devoted to creating the conditions for growth, success, and confidence in his students.

Paul remembers what transpired during his initial contacts with Joseph during a school music project:

"During the rehearsals, a very articulate boy named Joseph, using a voice device, told me that he couldn't sing. I was determined to find a way to get him into the songs and encouraged him to use his voice in his own way. The accuracy of the notes didn't matter as much as if he just made a joyful sound with us. That didn't sit well with this very soulful and intelligent boy. This dilemma stayed in the back of my mind for close to 6 months.

Joseph was later placed in my class for his senior kindergarten year. His group table was close to my desk, so I was treated to an unending dialogue of topics that included spies, war, theology, love and some very funny nonsense. At one point, I decided to begin saving some of the writings of this witty and profound child. That nagging feeling that I had to find a way for his voice to make it into music would not subside.

I went to ask a favor from my dear friends at the Ashley Ingram School of Music. I set up a meeting between Adrian Moody from the school and Joseph and his family. Joseph shared all of his lyrics with Adrian and completely captivated him with his soul, wit and brains".

That initial meeting with Adrian (AJ) at the studio was unforgettable. It was of course exciting, but I was a little uncertain about the whole thing – how could I take this seriously. Joseph had a handful of lines, hardly a cogent song idea, and we had no musical arrangement. Studio time is incredibly expensive and producers are very busy, so I thought why would anyone commit to this. Joseph was just 5 years old at that time, so I assumed this was all in the interest of humoring a little boy and his family. What else could I think?

What I didn't count on was meeting one of the most positive, talented, and generous people I have ever met. We were greeted at the studio door on a cold January morning by a cheerful and enthusiastic young producer. AJ was very warm and welcoming; treating us to a tour of the studio, complete with gold records on the walls and photos of some of the biggest pop stars in the world who had recorded there. AJ and Joseph hit it off immediately. It was obvious they were kindred spirits. Both fed off the other's enthusiasm and sense of humor, both completely fascinated by the other. There was no rush, no pressure to get in and get out. In one of the many rooms filled with instruments and gear, AJ treated Joseph to a demonstration of a variety of instruments including drums (traditional and electronic), pianos, keyboards and guitars – Joseph was in heaven, a kid in a musical candy store. After what seemed like hours, we entered the studio where AJ and Joseph would record together. I apologized for not having a clear musical idea or even a complete song and handed over Joseph's lyrics. Despite my trepidation, AJ was immediately excited and optimistic that something special was about to happen. Once again, there was a demonstration of the wall of recording equipment and computers in the room and then it was time to get to work – first transferring Joseph's lyrics as spoken by his computer into one of the studio computers, then a request from AJ for more lyrics.

"Ok, um...we'll get going and let you know when Joseph comes up with something and get back to you..." I said.

No, no, no Joseph, let's do it now, AJ said, "Gimme something" and Joseph responded. This was the best part of the whole experience for me, the sincere gesture of trust and respect AJ demonstrated toward Joseph in that moment. And with AJ's support and encouragement, Joseph delivered.

After all the lyrics were recorded, AJ demonstrated how he would manipulate the voice recording to make Joseph sing. This was, of course, a transformative moment...a moment where everything changed in an instant! I had never heard or imagined anything like it. In an instant, a world of possibilities opened up and a wall of limitation came crashing down. AJ Moody and Paul Alcamo had, without even realizing it, changed the world for Joseph and the multitudes that are sure to follow. Here is the experience in AJs words:

*"When Paul first approached me, he indeed sounded stumped. He had these fun and deep lyrics written by a 5 year old boy, but didn't know how to help him transform*

56

*them into song. I had no idea Joey had been diagnosed with CP, but only that he communicated through an electronic device. I had been trained to treat everyone in the studio as an artist and I was determined to approach this project with the same level of care and professionalism. When Joey and his family arrived, I knew that I wasn't just treating someone like a star: Joey is a star. He was engaged (more so than some professional artists!), energetic and was inspiring to work with. Using technology and software we often take for granted in the studio, I was able to work with Joey in creating a song that gave him his musical voice.*

*When we started out, I had no idea of the impact this experience would have on him, his family, his peers or myself. Joey taught me that expression is not about what we see or what we expect, but truly about being free to express what lies directly in our hearts. In fact, the result was so powerful to me, I quit my job and founded a nonprofit organization - Music Without Barriers - to help Joey and people all around the world find their voice, access music no matter the barriers, and give everyone the chance to shine. None of this could have been possible without people like Joey, his parents, Paul and the amazing community and staff at Holland-Bloorview. They say it takes a village; in this case it's true".*

Joseph presented his song "That Thing" at the Breaking the ICE (Independence Community and Empowerment) conference in Toronto in 2012. At just 5 years of age he introduced the song by saying he "wrote it to get rich" and was "still waiting", to uproarious laughter. When his song played, it literally brought the roof down. What Joseph, AJ and Paul accomplished together changed the lives of many of the people in the conference hall that day. It has that kind of power, and not just because it's a great piece of work for alternate communication users; it's a great song, period. And, at the heart of it is a young boy with a big voice, big ideas and lots of swagger. He just may represent a new beginning in what's possible and a new attitude in what's acceptable - for this generation and future generations of alternate communication user's.

The song "That Thing" is available on iTunes.

*Kevin Vieira*
*Toronto, Ontario – Canada*
*www.MusicWithoutBarriers.com*

## *"Kids for the Blues"*

This is a story of three girls, between the ages of 8 and 10 at the time, who were moved by the power of music to do something good. Their names are Norah and Ava (sisters) and their friend Kiley.

In August 2013, the girls and their families attended the annual Blues music festival held in Bean Blossom, Indiana. It was a hot evening, but the girls were the first ones to get up and start dancing to the music of Southern Hospitality, one of the featured bands that night. Then, the adults caught on, and soon it seemed like everyone was dancing in the crowd. These little girls were so full of energy, their enthusiasm was contagious!

The girls had a little cooler with their drinks in it, and when it was empty, people started walking by and tossing dollars in it. After a while, the girls ran over to their mothers and, with excitement, told them they had almost $35! Instead of candy or toys, they said they wanted to do something nice for someone. They knew about the campaign to build the Blues Hall of Fame and had one of their mothers write "Raise the Roof – All proceeds go to the Blues Hall of Fame" on their white container. The girls danced to the music for the rest of the night (almost 4 hours straight) and collected $50 to donate. It was a great night, but they didn't stop there.

The Blues Foundation found out about what the girls had done and posted about it on their website www.Blues.org. Soon after that, local radio personality, Penny Lane of WSVX Giant 96, heard about the girls and interviewed them on her radio show. She then asked them to write a song about that day. With the help of Norah and Ava's mother, Eve, they wrote a song that was recorded in the studio with Penny's son, Carson Diersing, and later played it on the air.

Vinny Marini, from the "Music on the Couch" radio show, heard the song and decided to use it as an intro to one of his BlogTalkRadio shows and had the girls on for an interview. Eve then started a Facebook page for the girls, as they wanted to continue gathering donations for the Blues Hall of Fame. Through Facebook donations and a few performances where they sang their song, the girls ultimately raised over $1,000.

The girls were then invited to attend the International Blues Challenge in Memphis, Tennessee in January 2014. While there, they had the opportunity to present their donation for the Blues Hall of Fame "Raise the Roof" Campaign to the Blues Foundation. They were each given plaques for their efforts by the Indiana Blues Society. But, the most exciting part of their trip was all of the amazing live music they were able to hear and the people they met. Amongst them were Eden Brent, Bob Margolin and Bob Corritore. Mr. Sipp, the 2014 IBC winner, became a quick favorite for Kiley. The girls were, again, interviewed by Vinny Marini during the IBC's for his Music On the Couch show. Bob Margolin heard they were doing the interview and came in to meet the girls before his show.

The girls were later invited by Jay Sielman, President and CEO of The Blues Foundation, to be presenters at the

2014 Blues Music Awards in Memphis, Tennessee in May. This was such a huge honor, as this was the first time any child or group of children have presented an award for the Blues Music Awards. They presented not only one award that night, but three! Best Male Soul Artist - John Nemeth, Best Female Soul Artist - Irma Thomas and Best Instrumentalist - Horn Eddie Shaw. Eddie was also inducted into the Blues Hall of Fame that same week!

Once again, the girls saw many musicians perform that weekend in both Memphis and Clarksdale; too many to even begin to mention. They made friends with everyone they met, and were walking on cloud 9 the entire time. This was absolutely an amazing opportunity for the three little music lovers.

We believe this is a great example of "no matter how small the person or effort, it can turn into something much bigger". It may, very well, be one of the best memories of a lifetime! It all started with three little girls dancing to the music they love, the Blues.

*Krista Hughes & Eve Bare*
*Morgantown & Franklin, Indiana – U.S.A.*
*www.Facebook.com/KidsForTheBlues*
*www.BeanBlossomBlues.com*
*www.Blues.org*

## "The Best and Most Beautiful Things in Life"

Our son, Michael, is 15 years old and a gifted piano player. While his gift brings so many people incredible joy, including him, how he came to appreciate music and develop his piano talent is anything but joyful.

When Michael was born, he was a very happy baby who loved all things musical: toys, cd's, mommy's lullabies. But, at just four months old, doctors admitted him to the hospital to try and find the cause of his shaking and swirling eyes. For 48 hours, through spinal taps, brain scans, test after grueling test, we played his favorite music (Mozart and silly children's songs) over and over. Through those 2 long days, the music greatly helped to soothe our little one. Eventually, the doctors would come to discover the medical reason for his symptoms: our son, Michael, was blind.

Over the next decade, Michael learned how to navigate a world he could not see with his eyes. Along the way, he developed a love for things he could feel, really feel, with his heart... and music is at the center of that. When the other kids his age were playing sports that he could not play, Michael took to the piano keys. When friends in middle school didn't understand his differences and pulled away socially from Michael, once again he took to the keys. While other teens were racking up scores on video games, Michael was racking up songs on his playlist as he explored his favorite genre, classic rock, and perfected that sound on both piano and keyboard. The interesting part is, Michael was never sad during any of this... he didn't wallow in the fact that he had so much time on his hands; it was as if he craved that time to better develop his talent...like this was time carved out for this specific purpose.

During their teen years, many blind kids are isolated from their peers because of the many social barriers that come with blindness. But, Michael is creating his own social opportunities by bringing people together with his classic rock band. He started a rock band program at his middle school, and coordinates incredibly popular open mic nights for tweens and teens that also act as fundraisers for our family's retinal research foundation (www.crb1.org). Michael also finds time to help out as musical/sound director (and actor!) in school plays.

When Michael was first diagnosed as blind, we initially worried if the community would have a place for him, how he would fit in socially and what obstacles would prevent him from achieving great things. Our worries have since faded as Michael's rock band, Casual Friday, has won numerous awards in our hometown, including best band in the county. He has been voted to Student Council in middle school and high school and people around town have even taken to calling him "The Mayor". But, most of all, Michael is best known for his passion and talent for music.

Music has carried Michael through some very difficult times. However, if you were to ask him, you can bet he would say he has carried a tune or two with him at all times; songs that allow him to see only the best and most beautiful things in life.

*Kristin Smedley*
*Bucks County, Pennsylvania – U.S.A.*
*www.MikeSmedleyMusic.com*

**There is MUSIC within each and every one of us.**

## *"Above Water"*

Although I didn't realize it until recently, music has always been a pivotal part of my fabric. I began playing piano and other instruments around the age of 5. However, I started singing before I can even remember. I began writing songs when I was 15, but not because I was groomed to be in the music industry or going for a record deal. It was simply my way of coping...living...and processing my world. Most of my family members knew I was musical, but quite a few didn't realize that I wrote songs until I landed a publishing deal when I was 17. What kept me alive wasn't the attention I got from music, but how the songs made me feel. It opened my thoughts and heart which, in turn, opened me up to relationships; family, friends and more.

I often feel the "gift of music" has been trivialized through the generations, with the notion that it's just entertainment; a hobby, a good pastime and nothing more. This amazing gift we've been given is certainly all of that and much more. Music, for me, was also a tool to keep going. What I mean by "keep going", is that it gave me purpose. I sometimes lose that sense of purpose, but music always brings that back for me.

There are a few inspiring stories I can remember during my musical journey so far, but one really stands out at the moment. I was recording my full-length record back in 2013, and even with my catalog of completed songs, I wasn't satisfied until I wrote one from scratch. With a little apprehension, I finished a song called "Above Water" addressing my depression. I honestly thought the recording of this new song would be just for posterity and represent a brave moment for me sharing my inner world. I certainly didn't expect it to be a favorite among listeners. However, several months after its release, I received a private message online from a fan and it read:

*"I'm going through depression right now and I just wanted to thank you for writing "Above Water". Your song stopped me from committing suicide. I was recklessly driving on the freeway and wanted to take my life away. Your song started playing and I just stopped myself when it touched something deep inside of me. Thank you for your music, from the bottom of my heart."*

I didn't quite know what to feel, so as graciously as I could, I replied and thanked her. This person put me in my place the moment I read their message. I, along with many others, was guilty of trivializing the very gift I'm given and the power it has on lives. It reminded me of that quote in a Spiderman movie, "...with great power, comes great responsibility." – cheesy yes, but truth, nonetheless!

The trajectory of my life, and how it's gone so far, would have been completely different without music. I probably would have been an architect or in the medical field, but thankfully the power of music pulled me in. I realize there are many who don't have the same "relationship" with music that I have - the passionate creative pursuit. But I believe we all can agree, accept and realize that it is meant to be kept alive - for the sake of the creators and music lovers, as well as, the casual listeners. Music is embedded inside all of us more than we'll ever really know.

*Melissa Polinar*
*Dallas, Texas – U.S.A.*
*www.MelissaPolinar.com*

## *"Breaking Down"*

Without music, I would be dead, there's no doubt in my mind. Music is what I did after I got sober. My song "Breaking Down" is a true life story. I needed something or somewhere to channel my energy and God provided it.

*Mini Thin*
*Weirton, West Virginia – U.S.A.*
*www.MiniThinMusic.com*

## *"The Greatest Gift One Could Ever Give"*

I began learning to play the piano at the age of five, and after thirteen years of private lessons, I went on to the Royal College of Music. I studied clarinet, orchestration, modern music and church organ. I also played in numerous bands throughout my teens including blues bands, dance bands and traditional jazz bands. Throughout my childhood I lived music every single day and indeed still do.

Growing up, there were many musical influences in my life. Eastern European composers, such as Prokofiev and Rimsky-Korsakov to name but just two. I listened to every kind of music I could and absorbed as many styles as I could. So many in fact, it would be impossible to single out any particular one. Even now, I am still listening and absorbing.

Over the years, I have witnessed many situations where someone needing help has found it through music. I believe that being able to transmit feelings to others through music is one of life's greatest gifts. There has never been a time in my life when music wasn't at the forefront. Music has always been pivotal in everything I have ever done both during the highs and the lows. I have always felt that music is probably the only language that can do this.

*Rick Wakeman*
*www.RWCC.com*

## *"In Honor of My Brothers"*

I was adopted at 10 months of age by the Weaver family, along with my older brother Aaron, and we grew up all over the state of Florida. Altogether, I was one of eight siblings and the youngest of three Weaver boys. When they reached adulthood, older brothers Steve and Aaron joined the military and attended flight school. When my time came, I decided to follow in their shoes. Three Weaver boys. Three Army Warrant Officers. Three helicopter pilots.

In 2004, my brother, Aaron was killed when the Medivac Black Hawk helicopter he was a passenger in was shot down by enemy fire in Iraq. At the time, I was also deployed in Iraq as a Black Hawk helicopter pilot. I definitely understood mortality and the risks of combat. After all, Aaron had survived the bloody 1993 battle in Mogadishu, Somalia that became the basis for the movie, Black Hawk Down. When Aaron died, however, something changed for me. I returned from combat and took a position training the next generation of Army aviators and officers at Fort Rucker, Alabama. I have not piloted a Black Hawk since that fateful day. Ten years after the last day I saw Aaron alive in Iraq, my brother-in-law, Randy Billings, was laid to rest one row back from Aaron. He was killed in action in Afghanistan on December 17, 2013 when the Blackhawk helicopter he was piloting was shot down by an enemy ground-detonated explosive device.

In July 2004, six months after the death of my brother Aaron, I went to a Jeffrey Steele concert at a local Alabama club. During the show, he performed a song titled "Nineteen," about a boy who joins the military and dies in combat at the age of nineteen. Hearing this song so soon after my brother's death really affected me, so I shared my personal story with Jeffrey when meeting him in the autograph line after the show.

In 2007, I began traveling to Nashville on a regular basis to write and record, and it was on one of those trips to Music City that I re-connected with Jeffrey Steele. I was thrilled that he not only remembered me, but also agreed to produce my recordings. The first song we recorded together was "Nineteen", which meant so much to me when I first heard it. Since then, Jeffrey has produced two more songs for me, "I'm That Guy" and "It's a Swamp Thang". I've also had the opportunity to record two of Jeffrey's songs, "January" and most recently, "New Set of Tires", which was co-written with Bob Dipiero and produced by Kimo Forrest.

I am now completely out of the Army and spend my time writing, recording and performing all over the country. I've been fortunate over the last several years to share the stage with several national acts, most notably, George Jones, Blake Shelton, Craig Morgan, Trace Adkins and Montgomery Gentry. One of my biggest thrills was when I recently opened for Charlie Daniels at the Ryman Auditorium. For me, it doesn't get much better than that.

Whenever I perform, I aim to connect with the crowd with a high-energy performance, delivering as much heart and soul as I can. I'm forever motivated to honor my two brothers who sacrificed their lives so I, and so many others, are free to chase our dreams.

*Ryan Weaver*
*Nashville, Tennessee – U.S.A.*
*www.WeaverCountry.com*

---

# MUSIC & LOVE: Two of the most beautiful gifts we can offer to the world.

---

## *"Man in the Mirror"*

I remember being on the Dangerous World Tour with Michael. We were playing at a huge soccer stadium in Germany. During the afternoon sound check, I wanted to hear what the band would sound like from the middle of the field, so I went out to listen. A minute later, a woman came up to me and introduced herself as Peggy, the personal assistant to the tour director, Kenny Ortega. She said, "Siedah, somebody just told me that you wrote 'Man in the Mirror.'" "Yeah, I did." "Wow! So you know Bill W.?" she asked. "Who? Bill W.? Who's he?" "Bill W. founded AA, and the lyrics to 'Man in the Mirror' sound like one of the tenets that he speaks of. You know, one of the Twelve Steps: Take a look at yourself and stop blaming others for your problems. I assumed you knew him."

Peggy went on to tell me how the song had affected her: "Last year was a really rough year for me. There were problems in my personal life, in my work, and I wasn't sure I wanted to keep on living. Then, I started really listening to 'Man in the Mirror,' over and over and over. You have no idea. That song stopped me from wanting to hurt myself, literally saving my life. I want to thank you so much for writing it."

There we were, standing in the middle of a soccer field in the middle of Germany, hugging each other and bawling our eyes out. That's when I realized just how powerfully pervasive music is, and how transformative a song's message can be. It really means something! "Man in the Mirror" proved to me that the ability to write songs is a gift much more powerful than I'd ever dreamed.

Long before I'd written anything that anyone had recorded, I had an eye-opening conversation with my then publisher about my songwriting goals. I shared with her that I wanted to write a song for Michael Jackson. She warned that I shouldn't set my sights that high. She shook her head and sarcastically quipped, "Yeah, you and every other songwriter in America!" I ignored her, and subsequently achieved a song placement with the biggest pop star in the world. Then, when it came time for Michael's follow-up album, Dangerous, I told her that I wanted to write, still, another song for Michael. Her response? "Come on, it happened once but, it ain't gonna happen twice!" I again ignored her pessimism and, subsequently, achieved a second Michael Jackson placement with song "Keep The Faith" on Dangerous, the BAD follow up album.

My publisher actually stopped speaking to me. Her negative attitude taught me that people often impose their own ceiling on your success. While you are under their ceiling, all is well, but the moment you break through and exceed their expectations, suddenly they get mad at YOU!

*Siedah Garrett*
*Los Angeles, California – U.S.A.*
*www.Siedah.com*
*www.InTheMirrorMusic.com*

## *"When Words Fail, Music Speaks"*

I believe that music is the only true international language that speaks to people of all different races, cultures and religious beliefs. A good piece of music will transcend time. I have been moved, emotionally, by music that was written hundreds of years ago. Listen carefully to the works of the masters: Bach, Mozart, Beethoven, Brahms, Schumann, Liszt, Chopin, and you'll soon see what I mean.

Music bridges generations. I remember being with my mother, and listening to the songs of Irving Berlin, Cole Porter, George Gershwin and Rodgers and Hammerstein...and I was an acne ridden teenager just dying to play her the new Beatles album: "Revolver" which, by the way, she really liked. Throughout my life, there were many artists who influenced me with their music. In no particular order they include Django Rheindhart, Charlie Parker, Jimi Hendrix, Eric Clapton, The Beatles, Stevie Wonder, The Stones, Robert Johnson, Maria Callas, Ray Charles, James Jamerson, Louis Armstrong, Buddy Rich, Otis Redding, Aretha Franklin, Chuck Berry, Muddy Waters, Buddy Guy, Jeff Beck and Frankie Miller.

Music has such a therapeutic effect on me and has helped me through many difficult times in my life. It is no secret, that in my early years, I struggled with addiction. In rehab, I was allowed to have a guitar, and as a form of therapy wrote several songs for the album "Seven Rays of Hope". This experience of expressing myself through these songs, helped me immensely with the healing process, and ultimately helped put my life back in the right direction.

One experience I will always remember, came some time ago, when I was in London participating in a drum clinic. It involved me talking about the drums and cymbals in my kit: explaining what each piece did and how the pieces worked together. The house lights were down and the stage was illuminated, so I couldn't really see the audience.

Whenever I banged a drum or tapped a cymbal, there was a clatter of clicks from somewhere in the back of the hall. It was kind of irritating, but was brief and not particularly intrusive, so I let it go. After my brief intro to the delights of the drum kit and drumming styles, I began to play a drum solo. I try to add light and shade to my solos. In the softer parts, I could once again hear a cacophony of clicks and bangs coming from the back of the hall. I gritted my teeth and played on, determined to chastise whoever was trying to disrupt me in my (brief) hour of glory. I came to the end of the solo and took a bow. The emcee thanked me and the audience clapped. Bizarrely, more clicks could be heard through the clapping.

Then, the lights went up. There, in the back of the hall, were about a dozen children in wheelchairs. They each had muscular dystrophy and, in their twisted hands, they held a pair of drumsticks. I jumped from the stage and began walking towards them, a lump forming in my throat. A lady walked towards me and thanked me for my lecture. She explained to me, that the children used drumming as a form of physical and mental therapy and hoped that their accompaniment didn't upset me in any way. I went to each child, and fighting back the tears, thanked them for coming.

I now work with teenagers battling addiction here in New York City. Through the power of music, I have seen kids who were sullen and uncooperative, transform over time, into happy participants...eager to pick up a tambourine or play a guitar or sing or provide lyrics.

Music has been my constant companion since I was a child. It has offered me hope and comfort in difficult times, has been a source of frustration and, more often than not, a beacon of inspiration. There are many quotes about the power of music, and here are two of my favorites: "Where words fail, music speaks" by Hans Christian Andersen and "Music from the soul can be heard by the universe" by Lao Tzu.

*Simon Kirke*
*New York, New York – U.S.A.*
*www.OfficialSimonKirke.com*

## *"You Get What You Give"*

My mother told me that when I was three, I once stared at a blade of grass for hours. She was worried I was autistic because, by the age of four, I still hadn't uttered a word. Truth is, my mind was simply so engrossed in absorbing life, that learning how to speak didn't seem to matter yet.

Growing up, listening to music became my spiritual solitude. When I heard the beauty and care that was possible in a piece of music, it became undeniably clear to me that, with the right amount of practice, I could use music to say everything I had in my rampant imagination.

When I was sixteen, I was a finalist on Canadian Idol, and had become a promising talent. Representatives in the music industry were taking interest and reaching out with their support. However, at the same time, I had also become numb to music...disenchanted and lost. I had accomplished a lot at a young age in the arts, but a voice in my head was constantly insisting that I would never top myself. I didn't want to make music, but I felt too guilty to give up and do something else. I would write and perform obsessively, more out of fear, rather than inspiration.

My self-esteem and energy plummeted. Very few people understood what I was dealing with. Eventually, I was diagnosed with depression. When therapy was proving insufficient, I resisted taking medication, so I wouldn't end up a 'zombie'. There I was, between a rock and a hard place - constantly bullying myself, but refusing help. If I tried to listen to music, it would quickly become an experience that would turn to self-loathing and self-inflicted violence. In my mind, if I couldn't enjoy music, then I had wasted my young life. I had skills with no purpose. I imagined myself becoming famous, and then dying at 28, like so many other self-destructive music figures before me. It seemed like the inevitable future. I had fostered a musical gift, but that same gift seemed to be killing me.

A few years later, a teacher at my university encouraged me to give to others when I felt like I couldn't get out of bed. Out of practicing generosity, even when I felt I had nothing to give, I started to develop a little bit of confidence.

About a year later I found myself in a personal development program, one that would allow me to make some sense of myself and find some peace of mind. As I sat in a room with 100 strangers, I watched and listened to a wise and energetic instructor, who in a previous life had been a Broadway dancer. He proceeded to take us through what felt like a Socratic dialogue regarding the human condition, led by a tap-dancing Gene Kelly. Having three non-stop days where I was made to face myself and confront my thoughts and dreams, was exactly what I needed...and far more than I could have imagined.

At one point, a participant got up on stage to try and justify how his mother was 'ruining his life'. Gradually, the program leader worked with him until he realized that he had made a ton of judgments about his mother when he didn't get his way as a child. Those instances had filtered his ability to see his Mom objectively as an adult. That's when it hit me: Life itself is a creative act. Like a song, we compose our points of view and how things appear to us. Just because some of the thoughts I have about myself (or others) aren't necessarily constructive, doesn't mean I have to take them as my truth. With this realization, I finally began to unravel the absurdity of all the things I had made up about myself and other people throughout my life. It was so obvious, that without doing some rigorous self-work, I couldn't see it. I was so creative, that not only had I written all of this music, but I had also written much of my own suffering throughout my life.

When I was thirteen, American Idol was the hot new TV program. A whole new generation of musicians were blasted with notions of 'making it big' at any cost and turning life into a competition. My innocent enthusiasm for music, amplified by the egocentricity that comes with the pursuit of fame, became a toxic combination that sucked the inspiration out from under my feet. I was convinced I was better than everyone else and was certain my over-confident, righteous mentality would bring me success. I now realized, I was responsible for the fact that I had stripped the joy out of music by making it all about success and glory. For the first time, I understood that I had bred my own suffering and began to experience myself as the boss of my own life. Nothing and nobody else was responsible for the quality of my life but me. I began to distinguish more inaccurate thoughts I had made up about myself (and others) and started making efforts to reconcile with people whose relationships with me had been affected.

Once I was actively reinventing my own life, most of my anxiety, depression, and inner-chatter faded away. Since my art was no longer just about me and trying to be famous, I was making my life much more about others. And trust me, 'you get what you give' is a very true saying. Just by shifting my mindset to give to others, my life has been filled with wondrous things. I am making a full-fledged living in the arts, on my own terms. I've written a musical, starred in numerous television shows as a voice actor, written music for television, I co-lead a songwriting workshop, I'm in a music duo with my best friend... and the list goes on. I've been a catalyst for positive transformations in others, as well as myself. And the cherry on top: if I ever made the time to do it, I'm sure I could (once again), have a very enjoyable afternoon just staring at a blade of grass, unafraid of the present moment.

Music bursts out of silence. In the same way, a life that bursts out of nothing – a life created moment by moment, free from the trials of the past – that is a life filled with the richest music of all.

*Taylor Abrahamse*
*Toronto, Canada*
*www.TaylorAbrahamse.ca*
*www.TaylorAndBryn.com*

## "Penny Shouts It Out!"

Penny is nine years old, and as she began this school year, she was a very shy child. She would never raise her hand to participate in a classroom discussion. While in third grade the previous year, she was even hesitant to talk to her teachers. Her conversations were limited to speaking quietly in very small groups or one-on-one with peers or a tutor. Up to this point in her school life, shyness had basically limited Penny's participation in any activity that might have helped her learn more and make more friends. If not for her learning disabilities, this good natured and cooperative student might have fallen between the cracks. Fortunately, Penny needed help with reading, so she was mine. I set my intention on finding a way to help her find the courage to shine.

Beginning this year, I was able to begin working with Penny in her class using a co-teaching model. I would come with Penny to her regular classroom for part of the school day, then also teach Penny for an hour a day, separate from the class, giving her additional academic support in a resource setting. When I first began to work with her, I realized that she was very hesitant to answer questions and never raised her hand to speak during group discussions. Even when working with her one-on-one, I found that she would wait a long time before answering a question. At times, I wasn't sure if it was her shyness preventing her from responding, or if she truly didn't know the answer. I looked for an opportunity to bring Penny out of her shell - something where she could be sure of herself by knowing the answers in advance. I felt that this would eliminate any confusion she might be having, and would help her receive encouragement from others. The answer finally came in the form of songs and a musical performance.

I enjoy writing children's curriculum-related poems and

songs, and sharing them with the teachers I work with. Through "Guitars in the Classroom", I began learning to put my poems to music and started to perform them with my students in special education classes. This year, our fourth grade is using math, grammar, reading and science songs to help teach these subjects and I am supplying much of the musical material. In Penny's group, I chose to use a series of poems and songs called PIE GUY. It is a series that begins on Halloween and reappears each holiday. I asked the four children in my special group to practice the poem and songs. We would then pick a day to perform them for their classmates, as well as, all three 4th grade classes.

The kids were so excited to practice, and the first performance was eye-opening. They loved memorizing the words and even changing their voices to act out the parts. However, when it came time to perform for their classmates, the whole lot of them clammed up. Almost all put the paper in front of their faces and whisper-read their parts. I guess when it came to performing, Penny was not the only shy child in the group. For her part especially, she read so softly and quickly, that I couldn't understand a single word she said. I'm sure the audience couldn't either.

I decided that for the next performance, I would get a microphone, keeping Penny's especially soft voice in mind. As each holiday approached, my students and I would practice the next piece in the series and then we would perform for the regular classrooms. The rest of my students were gaining confidence and their voices began to be heard, but Penny was still whispering. So, on Thanksgiving, I handed her the microphone and we all heard Penny's part perfectly! Technology had provided a great assist. But without amplification, Penny was still not audible. I wanted more from her and *for* her.

Upon our return to school in January, I presented a new piece and told the students we had just one day to practice before performing it the next day. They seemed excited and a little nervous too. I let the students practice in my room and was pleased that Penny read her part perfectly, yet, I still wasn't able to hear her very well. I had to find a way to help her get stronger without using a microphone, and fast. So, I took a chance and asked Penny to yell her part to me as I stood across the room. This request seemed a little strange, but I felt at this point, almost anything was worth trying. Her yell - her very loudest sound - was more like normal speaking...still, it was an improvement. We continued to practice this way that day and I lovingly teased her to scream at me! She giggled and got a little louder. The strength of our relationship and our growing bond, seemed to help encourage her to overcome her fear in these moments. The best part was, we could all see she was having fun! When her voice was finally audible across the room, I figured that was the best she would get. Besides, we always had the mic for the performance. Or so I thought.

The next day, we came to school ready to perform, only to discover the microphone had been dropped...and was now broken! Penny would have to do her performance alone, without assistance from the mic. If she could not speak out, her lines would cause a weak spot in the performance, and worse, her newfound confidence might begin to slip. The pressure was on! The kids were a bit nervous; prepping for this performance began to feel a lot like our very first one back at Halloween. I gave them a pep talk and told them their audience really wanted to have fun with them. Looking back, I think this made the difference - helping the children understand that the audience was not there to judge them, but rather to participate with them in the fun. Their challenge would be to get the audience involved.

To my surprise and relief, the performances were fantastic, and yes, even Penny got into the spirit! She held her head high, didn't cover her face with her paper, pronounced each word slowly and sang loudly enough for the kids in the back of the room to hear...*without* the microphone! I was so relieved for her and extremely proud of her at the same time. Penny had proven to herself and her classmates, that she could do her part...loudly, clearly and with conviction. She was able to let go of her worries and just have a great time. Turns out, all that shouting had paid off! I mean, if you can shout at your teacher, you can shout at anyone.

The kids were laughing when they came back to my room, eagerly chatting about what they would do for the next performance. Now they wanted to include costumes and were deciding what order they would go in. Penny was chiming in right along with the rest of them. A stranger would never have guessed how impossible this would have been just one month earlier. Practicing and then performing music with her classmates, and having permission to shout her loudest at me, has broken through Penny's limitations and improved her ability to participate more fully in class, and ultimately in life. She also now knows that an audience is not there to criticize her, but to encourage her to succeed. With all the negatives out of the way, Penny has truly begun to shine!

*Theresa Shoup*
*Georgetown, Kentucky – U.S.A.*
*Guitars in the Classroom*
*www.GuitarsInTheClassroom.org*

## *"Every Note and Lyric"*

I am a 13 year old singer, songwriter and pianist. Throughout my young career, I have had the pleasure of performing for audiences of all different ages and backgrounds. I have sung and played piano for special needs kids and for elderly residents in nursing homes. What I found, is that they all have one thing in common: Music touches and resonates in every one of them.

Music has the ability to uplift us whenever we are in the darkest of situations, and it is also there to help us express our feelings. Every note and lyric means something different to each person, but the effect it has is universal. Knowing I can make someone feel good by singing and playing music, makes ME very happy and thankful that we all have music.

*Valerie West*
*Broomall, Pennsylvania – U.S.A.*
*www.Valerie-West.com*

## *"Music is Magic"*

I think if you have even an inkling of a desire to play music, then you should protect that feeling and find a way to play, whether it's a hobby or a profession. Music is so personal. The way we listen, the way we play, the way we write. Music walks us towards comfort, truth and release. Every human deserves to feel those things. In a sense, music is magic.

*Vanessa Carlton*
*www.VanessaCarlton.com*

## *"Hop & Pull"*

It happened this week. It was a slight and simple change in my perspective that I've had for twelve years. I moved from a big city to the country twelve years ago and bought a horse. After all those years in office chairs, I've grown into a big man, and getting on the damn horse continued to be an embarrassment for me. First, I walked the horse like a dog on a leash. Then I found a big rock along the trail to help me get on the horse. Finally, I bought stairs. Believe me, those stairs allowed me to get my backside over the horse. I was finally able to ride and, consequently, I lost 28 pounds.

This past Tuesday, I woke up in a grumpy mood. You know, those kinds of days that we all have sometimes. I went to my computer and a customer email starts to frustrate me a little bit more. He was worried about deliveries. I'm thinking, oh God, is this ever going to end? I took a breath, and then remembered reading an article about an actor who used music to change his mood, allowing him to perform any kind of scene. So, what music could help me to change my grumpy, depressing mood, I thought? I needed something with a load of power, something explosive. Explosive? Yeah, dynamite, T.N.T.! So, I keyed up AC/DC's "T.N.T." and let it blast!

I listened to "T.N.T." all the way while driving from my house to my parent's house. I'm not a singer, but I sang along loud and very quickly found myself in an energetic mood. Upon arriving at the house, I continued to do my thing and prepared my horse "Gasoline" for riding. I saddled him up and then it was time to climb up those stairs like I've done a thousand times before. But, instead of climbing up, I looked at the stirrup. I contemplated. I said to Antonio, my ranch hand, "You know, I'm probably never ever gonna do this without the stairs. I can barely put my foot into the stirrup, let alone push my way up and over the horse." And he says, "No, no. All you do is hop and pull." "What?" I said. "Yes, hop 'n' pull."

At that moment, the way he said "hop 'n' pull" sounded a lot like "T. N. T." in the song. Then in just five seconds or less, as if TNT was exploding in my blood, I flew up onto the horse. I did it without using a tree, without using a rock, and without using the stairs. All I did was listen to the music in my head. It changed my mind. This accomplishment was a long time coming for me, and when I finally did it, it was kind of automatic. There was nobody cheering me on. Nobody said, "Wow, great!" I actually did it again to make sure I could repeat this long overdue "miracle".

On my way back to the office, I sang "We Are the Champions" all the way, to celebrate the victory over my own fears. I realized that, in the end, it was really, really easy. All I did was hop and pull. It changed my mind. Then I wondered...what else in my life do I need to change my mind about? What else *in my life do I just need to "hop and pull"?* WHAT ELSE IN LIFE DO I JUST NEED SOMEONE TO SING THE RIGHT SONG TO ME SO THAT I CAN DO IT?

*When you change your mind, what do you do?* Change your life.

*Wolfgang Gowin*
*Temecula, California – U.S.A.*
*www.wolf-gowin.de*

## *"It Takes a Village"*

Being born and raised in Venezuela, everyone in my family either played a musical instrument or sang. We were never given the choice of whether or not we wanted to be a musician. The choice we were given, was to pick what instrument we wanted to play.

When I was about 5 years old, I remember watching my great uncle play the guitar. One day, I tried playing the guitar myself, and my grandmother caught me. Her reaction was enlisting me in lessons the next day. And thus, my first instrument was the classical guitar. Because I was so small, I had to have a guitar made for me.

Soon after, I auditioned for the Jose Angel Lamas Conservatory, which is the oldest music conservatory in South America, dating back to the mid 1800's. By the time I graduated high school, I had been going to the music conservatory for 10 years. Despite my strong love of music, I decided to go to college for political sciences and international relations and received my Master's degree in international law. I never stopped playing music or singing, and my guitar was my constant companion. While in Europe during my Masters studies, I would sometimes go to the square or an Italian restaurant and play for money, although I mainly played music to escape the heaviness of politics.

After college, the second job I held in my career was working for the Venezuelan Consulate in Bonaire, a small island in the Netherlands Antilles. The total population of the island was, at the time, about 15,000...including the lizards and the donkeys. Needless to say, there wasn't much to do there. No theaters, no movies, nothing. And beside a few beach sports, there weren't many activities. Despite the beautiful scenery, you can only go to the beach so many times before you develop the need for change. I decided to start some sort of music program and began offering free lessons for kids to play the cuatro (a type of ukulele) at the Venezuelan Institute for Culture and Cooperation. After a year, I also started a musical theater class and taught 3 days a week. When I first put up a flyer for the classes, 10 kids came to register. By the end of the week, I had to take down the flyer and turn children away. There were too many students (47 to be exact) and not enough of me.

For our musical theater's first production, we decided to do "Beauty and the Beast", in Spanish, not too long after the Disney movie came out. There was no internet at the time to help with research. I sat down with my VHS tape & VCR and played it over and over while I transcribed the script...word for word, on paper. I also had to figure out how to transition various scenes. The materials to build the set and scaffolds came from a local construction project and were originally intended to be used to create the structure of a prefab building. Amazingly, the owner of the project just gave us all the materials out of the goodness of his heart. There was no budget for theater, but we managed to scrape together $500. There was also no theater to perform in. The only place with a stage was the local high school, which had no curtains, lights, sound or anything. Some close friends and local artists volunteered many evenings to build and paint the most amazing sets. The local radio & TV stations agreed to loan us microphones. A friend of the Ambassador, who was the general manager at the Harbour Village Beach Resort, offered to assist with the production and allowed us the use of all their landscape lights. He even gave us a crew of electricians to fabricate a lighting panel for the stage. Numerous parents of my students got involved with the project in ways that I could have never imagined. They helped with staging, blocking, running simultaneous rehearsals with me, transporting, feeding and caring for 47 kids between the ages of 2 and 15, lending time and love to a project that grew to be bigger than anything I could have imagined.

The Governor's wife got wind of what we were doing and asked how she could help. She felt this was something they should have been doing and wanted to assist us. She offered to make the stage curtains and costumes for all 47 children. Unfortunately, there were no fabric stores in Bonaire, so the Harbour Village Beach Resort ended up with 17 missing sheets...and guess where they went? Yes, to the curtains at the high school! After sewing the sheets together to make the curtains, the Governor's wife found herself trapped in a sea of blankets impossible to fold. She had to wake up her husband (the Governor), their children and their entire staff at 3:00 in the morning to help fold the curtain...it was so massive that they actually took it out to the street to fold it. We also didn't have a lot of fabric to make costumes, so the Governor's wife made Belle's Ball dress entirely of yellow paper. It was absolutely beautiful!

The Governor made it a "mandatory suggestion" for all the teachers and students to go to the play. He even gave a speech about musical theater and talked about how you can do anything if you really put your mind to it. When I originally thought of the musical theater idea, I was told it was impossible. But, I'm one of those people who becomes even more interested in doing something when it seems to be "impossible ".

Creating this program changed a lot of kids' lives, as well as mine. Many of the kids went from having nothing to do, to being on stage. We took kids off the street. Kids that never thought they would amount to much, found themselves acting, singing, dancing, memorizing the long dialogues of a 2 and a half hour long script. We gave them a new perspective, and with that, we opened possibilities in their lives.   The program also changed the lives of all the adults involved in it. We found our sense of community, for the sake of the children. Me? I found my true calling in life: working with children. By far, this was one of the most important and incredible things I have ever done in my life. I gave it months of work and sleepless nights. It cost me a lot of arguments with people that "didn't get" how important it was for me and everyone else involved. When it was all said and done, it wasn't me, but all of Bonaire who made it possible, In the end, it really did take a village!

*Yosmar Salazar-Márquez Vinson*
*Brookhaven, Pennsylvania- USA*
*Musician*

### "The Gift of Music"

We may have lost our heart to heart connection to the cyber world, but GOD blessed us all with the gift of music; a gift to help us to forever touch one another's soul.

*Ziba Shirazi*
*Los Angeles, California – U.S.A.*
*www.ZibaShirazi.com*

> # *Music is the Universal Language and is perhaps the Greatest Gift the Universe has ever given us.*

# *Musical*

# *Memories*

Some days, everyone's a critic!

## *"One Note at a Time"*

I grew up in the 70's when movie musicals were all the rage, including many of the children's variety. Anyone remember Chitty Chitty Bang Bang or how about Bedknobs and Broomsticks? And who could forget Disney's Fantasia, the first-ever music video blending orchestral works from some of the great masters with Disney's imaginative visuals. Music and sound, more generally, captured my attention at a very early age, holding sway over my mood and sparking my desire to hear more. One day, my mother had two movers roll a Whitney upright piano into the bedroom that my brother and I shared. I'm not sure whether she sensed some early innate ability in me (I was only 3 years old), or was it part of a grand plan to ensure all three of her children grew up cultured and aware of the arts; to help ensure we all had a better shot at making our way in this world than she did.

When it arrived, I immediately plunked on that piano one key at a time. Most kids would delight in moving their whole arm over the black and whites and being rewarded with a happy jumble of sound. No, not me; I was always keenly happy to just listen to the particular vibration each note made, and for how long I continued in this way, I can't recall. But, I clearly remember the first time I played two notes together, and was surprised to hear that third sound – you know what I mean – where the result is more than either individual note. That discovery kept me busy for a very long time! So it was in this way, by listening slowly, I gradually began my introduction to the instrument. My ear was always my guide. Being a kind of absent-minded kid who's thoughts were elsewhere and didn't understand structure, I gravitated towards improvising rather than grasping the analytical fundamentals of music. To this day, I think my ear was both a blessing and an impediment, but that's a story for another day.

What I want to convey to you is how consuming musical sounds, really any sound, was to me. I remember once being simultaneously enthralled and pained to hear an achingly beautiful song accompanying a 1969 video on Sesame Street; I was 4 years old and the video showed rain falling on beautiful green leaves outside a slightly opaque window. The song was Vivaldi's Guitar Concerto in D Adagio. I almost couldn't watch; the music was so sad and moving. This is how it was for me with many sounds, especially nature sounds like the wind through trees; a sound which exhilarates me even today.

Fast forward to grammar school, possibly 8th grade, when a winter storm hit and I got to stay home. My nascent recording career was heating up; I had just purchased 2 Shure microphones and my very first tape deck from Radio Shack. I had been eyeing that tape deck for a very long time and was finally able to afford it, thanks to my paper route (remember those?). Adding to my "studio" was a monophonic synthesizer and the coup de grâce – my father's Fisher stereo system and his prized Denon tape deck (both of which were strictly off-limits, mind you). To record multiple tracks, I did the old trick of bouncing music tracks between tape decks for a gloriously happy song that gave me goosebumps when I listened back. I named my new creation "Winter Storm", in honor of Mother Nature's gift to me. The feeling of being able to create a song that I loved to listen to, even more than anyone else's music, was transformational for me. I wanted nothing more than to create music, because that's when I felt most at home and most at ease, where everything else was a muddled confusion – school, social awareness, family. I guess what turned out to be a moderate case of ADD (not discovered until my 40's) actually helped focus me on my music.

Growing up, my entire grammar school and high school experience would have crushed me, were it not for music.

Music gave me the confidence to know that I was actually good at something. Perhaps, just as importantly, it gave me a safe haven when all around me the world was a scary place and nothing seemed in my control.

Music was always my calm and my peace; well, except for when my mom would just lose it after hearing me bang out my frustrations with repetitive patterns on the piano. That noise would have driven a saint crazy, so she would yell at the top of her lungs for me to stop. In retrospect, that was quite funny!

*Andre Maranhao*
*Aston, Pennsylvania – U.S.A.*
*www.AndreMaranhao.com*

## "Best Education I Ever Received"

While growing up in Jamestown, New York, I went to public school and was constantly bullied and teased by neighborhood kids who went to a parochial school. Apparently, they thought I was an "outcast" and would gang up on me when I walked home from school, hitting me or pushing me down to the ground. It really wasn't until I started playing music that I finally began to feel accepted for something.

My parents bought me a trumpet, because I loved the sound of the big band music they played at home. Somehow, the trumpet was the sound I identified with, and I was just seven years old when I began taking lessons. From there, I played in the school bands and by age 13, I had my own little combo. By the time rock and roll came out, my confidence through music had grown to where I was no longer afraid of the bullies. I was able to get out into the world, have many more friends and had a great time playing music at schools, VFWs, the Moose Club and many other venues.

After graduating college, I began my teaching career at Sharon Hill High School in the Philadelphia area. This was a blue collar town with a tough environment and a lot of rough kids. There were drug problems and motorcycle gangs. Since I was young and tall, the school gave me some of the more difficult classes. Many of the students in my classes had some of the hardest home lives. I needed to find a way to help reach these kids. I was teaching poetry in English class and, one day, I brought my guitar to school. I began to play songs by The Beatles, Simon & Garfunkel and other popular artists of the day to demonstrate the lyrics in the songs and how they related to poetry. For the very first time, I saw the kids' eyes light up as they began to see art and poetry in a whole new way. I have to chuckle now, because after that, the kids began to think I was the cool teacher. We even put on a school concert where I played along with several student musicians playing bass, drums and guitar. Many of the kids and I became very close through this whole experience and I know it changed us all. I eventually stopped teaching in order to pursue music and, later, one of my former students played drums in my band.

Since that time, I've played music my entire life. At one point in my career, I was playing in nursing homes and assisted living facilities several times a month. One day, while playing at a local nursing home, I was performing songs from musicals including Oklahoma, Carousel and others. I started to play songs from the musical South Pacific, when all of a sudden I heard this most beautiful voice coming from somewhere in the room. I'm looking around and can't see where this voice is coming from. To me, it honestly sounded like an angel from the other side. The Activity Director quickly came over to me and urged me to keep playing. I went from one song to another for 10 to 12 pages. The beautiful mystery voice knew all the lyrics and continued to sing right along with me. All the other employees, nurses and doctors came in to see what was happening. When I finally stopped, the whole facility was going crazy. They said "Jay, this is a miracle! There is a lady named Edith, in her 90's, who has not spoken or sang for months and months. She used to sing off-Broadway and when she came to the nursing home, she would sing until her Alzheimer's condition got worse. We can't believe it – she knew every lyric and every word and her voice was absolutely gorgeous."

I went to find Edith and found her sitting in a wheelchair in the corner of the room. I said "Edith, what a beautiful voice you have, I want to thank you". I touched her hand, but her head remained down and there was no response. When the music stopped she had once again shut down. The facility's doctor came over while I was packing up my equipment and said "Do you know what we have witnessed here? Studies have shown, that the last thing that goes in a person's memory when they start to lose it, is lyrics and melodies". I realized right then and there, that anybody who doesn't think music has tremendous power is crazy. This was one of the most beautiful experiences of my entire life. Music is, without a doubt, the best education I ever received.

*Bluesman Jay Gullo*
*Philadelphia, Pennsylvania – U.S.A.*
*www.youtube.com/user/TheBluesmanJay*

## "Anyone Here Play the Banjo?"

I had known for years that I wanted something unique and way more exciting than a traditional job in my hometown and I couldn't wait to get started. In my senior year of high school I signed up with an Army Reserve Unit and began attending weekly training sessions at my local armory. The military draft was still in force and I always felt a sense of patriotism and loyalty to my country. I realized I could start pursuing my dreams, and at the same time, begin serving my country by attending weekly training sessions and two-week summer camps that would go on for seven years.

So, the day after high school graduation, I promised my love forever to Becky Brill, my childhood sweetheart, said a very final "goodbye" to my mom, dad and two sisters on the tarmac of the Phoenix Sky Harbor Airport and boarded a twin engine Douglas C-53 for Fort Ord, near Monterey, California, to begin my six months of active duty.

During my first eight weeks of basic training, I remember the drill sergeant pushing me and the rest of the recruits all day long to the limits of our endurance. There were endless runs through desert trails, thick with choking dust, crawling across barbed-wired infiltration courses while live bullets whizzed above our heads. Then there were forays into tear gas-filled buildings without a gas mask. But more terrifying than the bullets and the gas was my loneliness and being an introvert surrounded by a platoon of strangers.

More than anything, I think I survived those grueling weeks by listening to Little Richard, Sam Cooke, and Elvis Presley on the local radio station in the evenings and by reading Becky's letters that arrived almost daily. I remember folding one of her letters and slipping it into the chest pocket of my t-shirt to keep it near my heart.

I was discharged just in time to spend the holidays

with Becky and my folks. I then caught a ride to California with my high school buddy, Benny, who was on his way back to college in Pasadena. Benny dropped me off at the corner of Hollywood and Vine on New Year's Day, 1958. I was eighteen and I had come to seek my fortune. I set my duffle bag on the curb and checked my pocket to make sure they were still there: two twenties and a ten.

I soon landed a job printing record labels, and my walk to work every morning took me past a theater-style marquee that hung over the door of a small recording studio on Vine Street where someone had arranged the letters to read, "Come In & See What Your Voice Sounds Like – $10." Every day, as I passed by, the sign would silently call to me. I'd sometimes turn and look back at it as I walked on. After a few days, I became intrigued by the sign and its implications. Soon intrigue turned to obsession!

One Saturday morning I got up my nerve and booked ten dollars worth of studio time. My heart pounding, I started with something I knew I could do: I laid down a Jerry Lee Lewis style piano track. Then, by sheer willpower, I forced myself to over dub some background vocals and sang lead on my version of "You Are My Sunshine." Although I was totally unaware of the musical influences that were flowing out of my mouth and into the microphone, as I look back, I'm sure they must have been a combination of the great country, black gospel, and rhythm and blues artists that had brought such joyful feelings into my young life—everyone from Fats Domino to Ricky Nelson.

When the sound engineer signaled me into the control booth I could feel my face turn beet red, but when he played the record back for me, I couldn't believe my ears. He had equalized the tracks and blended my voices together with tape echo. A wave of excitement broke over my fantasy that the tape sounded like a record I might hear on the radio. From that moment I was hooked. It was only weeks before I was spending every Saturday, and nearly all the money I was earning at the print shop, making music at Fidelity Recorders.

One day, a fellow stuck his head in the door of the studio and asked, "Anyone in here play the banjo?" I raised my hand involuntarily and managed a shy, "I do." I quickly stifled the flutter of apprehension that I might not be able to fulfill the man's expectations and followed him down the street to Music City, the famous music store on the corner of Sunset and Vine where the man rented a tenor banjo. Then he took me to another little studio across the street from Fidelity, where he set up a microphone and instructed me to strum along on the banjo as I sang "Red River Valley" and "Oh, Susanna." More than likely, it was a lucrative movie or TV background score for the producer, but he handed me a ten spot after the session and I left with my head in the air. "Yippee!" I thought to myself, "I just turned professional!"

I had many experiences growing up where music influenced me, but one of my favorites was in my teens when, our minister would often call on me to play the church piano or the Hammond B-3 for the congregational singing. Almost as often, he would admonish me afterwards to tone down the rock 'n' roll treatment I'd be giving to the old hymns. I had found the passkey to more fully expressing myself. From the twist clubs of 1962, through my career as a hit songwriter and record producer for The Monkees and other pop stars, up to the present when I play on Sundays at my local church, the Hammond B-3 organ has been my instrument of choice ever since.

*Bobby Hart & Glenn Ballantyne*
*www.OfficialBoyceandHart.com*
*www.GlennBallantyne.com*

## "Who Sings That Song?"

My dad gave me my love of music, as well as my knowledge of music. I can remember car rides with my dad behind the wheel and my brothers in the backseat. A song would come on and dad would say "A dollar to whoever can name the group". If no one knew the group on the first guess, he would give us a hint, but knock a quarter off the reward. It was in these car rides where I learned about the great doo wop groups and the incredible songs they recorded. It was always a great feeling when I would know one of the more obscure groups and surprise my dad with the right answer. He would exclaim "Very nice!" and it would put a big smile on my face.

I am now in a band called The Wayside Shakeup and my dad is our biggest fan. He learns all the words to our songs, comes out to every show and has even sang backing vocals on a few of our studio recordings. Music was, and will always be, one of our strongest bonds.

*Chris D'Antonio – The Wayside Shakeup*
*Haddon Township, New Jersey – U.S.A.*
*TheWaysideShakeup.com*

---

## Looking to boost your brain power?

Try picking up a musical instrument! Research has shown that musicians have better language processing skills and enhanced working memory when compared to non-musicians.

---

## "Unforgettable"

When I was a kid, the popular music of the day was big band and jazz. They used to have what they called canteens, places where we danced to slow music and the jitterbug. Some of our favorite artists at the time were Stan Kenton, Tony Bennett, Frank Sinatra, Nat Cole, Billy Eckstine, Vawn Monroe and the Les Brown Orchestra.

In 1951, I was 17 years old, and on one Saturday night me and a couple of my buddies were on the corner in Drexel Hill where we hung out. We got to talking and decided we were gonna dress up and go down to Club Harlem in West Philadelphia to see the Nat King Cole Trio. We put on our shirts and ties that we wore back then, along with our Billy Eckstine collars, and headed off to the club. Club Harlem was a nice club, and we were the only 3 white boys in the place...we felt like the inside of an Oreo cookie. Everyone was very friendly; it was great to see that music was the only thing that mattered. It was an excellent show and so much fun to see Nat Cole before he made it big as a solo artist. Back then, it was just Nat on the piano, along with a guitar player and stand-up bass. There were many of Nat's songs that we loved including "Route 66", "Nature Boy", "Mona Lisa" and "Too Young", which went to #1 that year. Also in 1951, was the very first release of his signature song "Unforgettable". Later, he went on to host his own TV show on NBC for several years. Nat King Cole was the epitome of slow dance music, and the night we saw him in that little club is something I'll always remember.

*David Charles*
*Media, Pennsylvania – U.S.A.*
*www.CustomLeisureTravel.com*

## "The World of Harry Chapin"

Many of us have been touched by the beautiful songs and magnificent story telling of Harry Chapin. His efforts to help further important social causes in our world were also well known. Most of us, however, will always remember Harry for two very special songs. The first, "Taxi", masterfully tells the tale of a couple's poignant, if brief, reunion after separating long ago. The second, "Cat's in the Cradle" was a #1 hit in 1974, and reminds parents everywhere that we need to find more time to spend with our children when they're young. Harry tragically left this world before the age of 40. What follows is a brief anecdote courtesy of Howard Fields who, for seven years, was the drummer for Harry Chapin and currently plays alongside Harry's brothers Steve and Tom.

My seven years performing with Harry began with a 1975 Broadway show entitled "The Night That Made America Famous". The show was based around Harry's music and starred Harry. One of my favorite memories of him occurred on the night of March 1, 1975. Both of our Saturday performances were complete when Harry entered the band dressing room and asked Big John, Harry's bassist and backup singer, if he would like to attend the Grammy Awards with him. The ceremony was being held that night, just a few blocks away at the Uris Theater. Harry had been nominated that year as Best Male Vocalist for "Cat's In The Cradle" and was also performing the song that night. Harry had one extra ticket for the event, and after John politely declined, Harry then put the ticket up for grabs. Only after it appeared no one else was taking it, I found myself in a cab with Harry, his wife Sandy and his dad Jim...rushing over to the Grammy's, which had already begun. As we entered the building and approached the doors leading from the lobby into the actual theater, a young usher (about 20 years old) noted that Harry was overburdened with a guitar (not in its case), a leather bag and one or two other items. The usher offered to take the guitar, which Harry gladly gave up. Then, somehow, as the usher was holding the guitar and at the same time attempting to open the theater door, he dropped the instrument and then tripped in such a way that one of his feet came down right on the guitar. So, there the guitar lay... smashed on the ground. It happened in a nano-second and it wasn't pretty. All I remember at that point, was Harry putting his arms around this devastated and horrified kid and saying to him "Don't worry about it bro". Harry could be like that. End of story.

A few minutes later we were seated, when all of a sudden, Harry got up. He walked about eight rows back in the theater to where Gladys Knight & The Pips (who were also up for an award) were seated. He said a few words to them and then returned to his seat. Harry's wife, Sandy, asked him what that was about. Harry replied "I just told them what a great line I thought 'I'd rather live in his world than live without him in mine' was" (from "Midnight Train To Georgia"). I took note, at that moment, about the art and power of great lyrics and how that really made Harry tick.

*Howard Fields*
*Drummer, Harry Chapin Band, 1974-1981*
*www.HowieFields.com*

## "Changing the Course of History"

I am a native Philadelphian, career musician of 30+ years and very proud of my title as musician, percussionist or band leader, as I am often called. The journey has been both challenging and rewarding. I was a mediocre student in elementary school with very supportive parents. As a child I played sports and took piano lessons, but was average, at best, and uninspired by most things. Like most kids, I had tremendous energy and a thirst for knowledge, despite my ability to become easily distracted.

I was in 3rd or 4th grade when a quartet of local jazz musicians performed an assembly program at my elementary school (the Greenfield School). They were the Gerald Price Quartet: Tony Williams on saxophone, pianist Gerald Price, bassist Benny Nelson and Al Jackson on drums. Tony Williams is the only surviving member and remains a friend and mentor. That one performance was a pivotal moment in my young life. From that experience, I began to tap out rhythms on everything I could find. I even dusted off my parent's old record collection and listened to each album over and over again. I learned the history of a rich musical culture called Jazz, read books on the topic, attended concerts and convinced my parents to provide me with music lessons. I sought out music icons, met them, studied them and took lessons with many of them. By the time I was 15, I began to perform with, and develop friendships with, numerous musicians of my parents' generation. Before long, I was widely considered a protégé and received much acclaim.

Post high school, I embarked on a long career that includes touring, recording, theatre and teaching. I have been a roster artist for Musicopia, where I am now beginning my 8th year. I would like to think, that along the way, I have also influenced my share of aspiring young musicians. I have performed with many well-known recording artists and could drop dozens of names. However, I am equally proud of my students' accomplishments as well, and will name a few of them instead including:. Amir Thompson (drummer with The Roots, and currently leads The Tonight Show band); Auri Hoenig (amazing Jazz drummer and composer living in NYC); Marcus Walls (percussionist working on Broadway and touring); and my two sons Leon Jordan, Jr. (trumpeter, composer, UARTS Grad and educator.); Jovon Jordan (percussionist, composer and Musicopia roster artist).

Sometimes all it takes, is a single musical performance to profoundly influence a life, and perhaps, change the course of history.

*Leon Jordan, Sr.*
*Philadelphia, Pennsylvania – U.S.A.*
*www.RenaissanceOrchestra.com*

## *"Feel the Magic in Your Life"*

My dad was a world famous concert violinist. From the time I was in the crib, I would hear him always practicing... either for a concert or just keeping up his technique, day in and day out. By the time I was 3 or 4 years old, I played around on the piano and then off I went to lessons. By the time I was 14, I became my father's regular accompanist and did concert tours with him all over. That's how I came into music. I developed a wonderful career and life because of music and I am so very thankful for it. I see it being very difficult for young musicians in this day and age to have that kind of success. There will always be someone who breaks through and has a hit record. But, Madonna and Lady Gaga are one in a million...they are really smart business people; they have made millions fast and will retire with a big bank account. However, most others will not be so fortunate, at least from a financial point of view.

There are a lot less musician jobs available today. Back in the 1960's, The Wrecking Crew guys were making really good money. But, there were very few musicians who could do what they did, as well as they did it (at that level). As a studio musician, I had to look at music and be able to play that song in 5 minutes like I had been playing it for 20 years, no matter the key or how complicated it was. It took me years of dedication, talent and luck to get to that level. I was fortunate to be in the right place at the right time. My stars aligned and things started happening for me. It wasn't easy...I had my struggling years (tomato soup made from ketchup and flour balls). But, if I had followed my classical piano career, I was pretty much guaranteed a place. I didn't care for classical though. It wasn't really what I wanted. When I was 14 years old, I began gravitating towards popular music. I literally threw away my classical career, much to the chagrin of my father...it was very hard on him. Instead, I went into rock 'n roll and, through that, became a very successful studio musician. I wasn't aiming at a studio musician career; I was aiming to be the star! I wanted to be the next Roger Williams. I wanted to be a solo recording artist. Either fortunately or unfortunately, I don't know, I never did catch that hit record. I had a lot of records out, but not "the one". I became a musical director and arranger and then record producer. I just kept changing and evolving as the world led me.

In 1967, I was asked by Johnny Mathis to be his musical director. He was doing a European tour...it was my first serious musical directing job. In 1969, Nancy Wilson hired me as her musical director. Because of what I was doing, working as a studio musician, I played on every

Sonny & Cher hit record that there was. Then, in 1971, when Sonny & Cher got their TV show, I became their musical director. So, while I was a studio musician, I was also going on the road and doing these other wonderful things. I was very, very fortunate. People were happy with my work, so I continued to get great jobs. This led to being asked to score my first movie around 1980. It was a musician's dream job. I liked it so much that I went out and got an agent! That became my main occupation from about 1980 to 2000. I had a great twenty-year run, but decided I had done enough, so I retired from that in 2000.

Now, there are so many people working on films, you never see the same person's names on the composing credits anymore. There are always different composers being used for different movies...there is very little loyalty from the producers. The competition is too great...so much so, that the producers take advantage and now pay a 10th of what they used to pay for music. As a result, much of the music in films these days sound so much the same. Hopeful composers are pretty much submitting demo tapes that sound so much alike. It's like they are using the same sequencers, the same sound modules to get their sounds, and often using the same basic 3 chords. Even the most accomplished composers are now using the "Ivory Orchestra" synthesizers for their orchestral scores. The musicians they used to use aren't playing anymore, there's not enough work available. This trend started back in the late 70's. When modern synthesizers first came on the scene, the big string section players were the first to go. It was cheaper to replace a string section with a machine. It actually all really started back in the 40's and 50's with the advent of the electronic organ. Even the oldest organ has buttons on it for violin, clarinet, oboe, cello, etc., and the concept was to replace or imitate certain instruments. It put a lot of people out of work. There are very few producers who will use a real orchestra today...it's just more cost effective to use a synthesizer. But then, the writing of scores is bound to the limitations of the synthesizers, which can't duplicate what a real live orchestra does...it's not the same exact sounds. There is always a type of artificial sound with music being played with a synthesizer. Sadly, most people can't even tell the difference anymore...it has become "the norm". This is all the kids know today, unless they are musicians and play a real instrument.

Not having music education in schools is a huge mistake...it needs to be valued. Not having arts education means turning out a society that doesn't know anything about art, whether it is painting, music, dance, etc. Not having music education is damaging to society and very unfortunate. They are sending out into the world, a personality that is not completely formed...like only 70 to 80% formed; they are missing the whole artistic side of their life. The arts help develop the brain. Many school systems don't understand the significance of music and don't place enough importance on the arts. Imagine if schools were to teach music and art in place of sports activities...our whole society would be different. You would have more people dancing and playing real music. We would all be happier, but people only get what they are exposed to.

My final thoughts for kids today: Pick up an instrument and learn how to play...follow through and you will see the magic that will happen in *your* life. Do it for fun, do it to feel good, but don't quit your day job.

Good luck,

*Michel Rubini*
*Palm Springs, California – U.S.A.*
*www.MichelRubini.com*

## "Hard Days, Hard Nights"

My father came to America from Pescara, Italy when he was 17 year old. He immediately began working in the coal mine, until he met and married my mother. My grandfather then got him a job at Westinghouse Electric and his life got a whole lot better. Mom and Dad had ten of us kids, and Dad never made more than about $50 a week. We were poor, but never knew it. We lived in a two-bedroom house with my four brothers and I living in the attic. There was no heat or hot water in the attic until I was about 8 or 9. The best any of us could hope for when we grew up was to go to work in a nearby coal mine or factory.

As early as I can remember, the only music that was played on the radio in our house, was when dad listened to Puccini, Verdi or the great Italian classics, like the songs you hear the great tenors sing even today. That is probably what influenced Dad to buy me a violin when I was in second grade. Mom told me to take good care of it, because Dad still owed the man at the music store the $100 that it costs. Dad agreed to pay $2 a week.

Mom arranged for me to take lessons from the school's music teacher, Mr. Darr, right after my school classes. I was very excited to learn how to play that beautiful instrument and was very careful to place it on that red velvet cloth inside the case.

On the day of my first lesson, I followed my mother's instruction and was very careful with the violin. After the lesson, I walked outside the school and down the steps that led to the street below, where a group of boys were playing football. We didn't have playgrounds in those days, so we played on the street. When the boys saw me, they immediately formed a circle around me and started teasing and punching me. They grabbed my instrument case, took the violin out and started tossing it around. They punched me and my glasses fell off and broke. Before I knew it, I had a bloody nose and was down on the ground being punched and kicked and made fun of. They told me I was a sissy for playing the violin instead of football. I was crying, not from the beating I was receiving, but because I realized I had not taken care of the violin as I promised.

Fortunately, for me, Mr. Darr was done for the day and when he came down the school steps and saw what was going on, he yelled for the boys to stop and they ran away. Mr. Darr helped me find my glasses and put the remnants of the violin in the case, and then offered to drive me home. When I walked through the door, my entire family was sitting at the kitchen table waiting for me so we could eat dinner together. Remember those days?

When my mother saw me, she started crying. Everyone got up from the table in shock. My brother Ralph (the tough guy in our house) wanted to go out and get revenge, but my father said to just let it go and forget it. I asked Dad if I could quit taking any more music lessons. He agreed and that ended my career in music, at least for a while.

About 6 years later, my oldest brother (nicknamed JuJu) joined the Marine Corp and that left his accordion for me to play. I was so proud of my brother for becoming a Marine. World War II had been over for only a few years and my oldest brother (I was the baby boy) would always tell me that the greatest thing that we could do was to offer to die for our country. I was only seven or eight at the time, but I wanted to be just like my brother... I wanted to be a Marine.

About a year after JuJu left home and entered the Marine Corp, he was home on a 30-day leave. He was up on a ladder painting the exterior of our house when the phone rang. My mother answered it and heard the news that she feared for all of her five boys. "JuJu", she yelled, "Come down. It's the Marines, the North Koreans invaded South Korea. You have to leave for Korea immediately." Mom cried that day. Her biggest fear was that her five sons would get killed while off at war. After all, the big war was just over a few years ago and many of the boys in town had been killed overseas. Of mom's five boys, she had two marines, one in the Coast Guard, one in the National Guard and another son in the Army. We had gone through the Korean War and Vietnam War and we were all very fortunate to have survived. We were also very proud when JuJu received a purple heart.

With my brother off to war, I continued my music lessons, this time on his accordion. We all missed the sound of the accordion in the house and playing it helped me feel closer to him. After that, I would learn to play any instrument that I could get my hands on and music became very important in my young life.

Growing up, the holidays were special in our neighborhood, especially Christmas. Even though all of our neighbors were poor, we celebrated Christmas with lots of food. Everyone baked and went all out with the best of food and, of course, music.

On Christmas Eve, it was an Italian tradition to have the feast of seven fishes. Every family filled their dining room tables with food and baked goods, and all of the neighbors walked from door to door to celebrate together. Nobody bothered to knock, you just went to everyone's house to visit and to eat and drink, and music was a big part of the celebration.

Patsy Morocco, playing Christmas carols on his accordion, would lead the parade of people singing throughout the neighborhood to well past midnight. You didn't need an invitation; all you needed was to be in the true Christmas spirit. We never expected presents, nor did we get any. The real highlight of the night was when our barber Dom Caruso visited, and he gave each of my brothers and me the only Christmas present we would receive, a half dollar coin. I truly loved those Christmases.

When I graduated from high school, I didn't want to get a job in one of the factories where almost everyone else in town worked. I told my father, "I want to make a living working in the music business." Dad said, "You can't do that. Nobody makes a living playing music." But, I was very fortunate. I had a father who believed in me and he agreed to let me give it a chance.

I wrote 2 songs that were recorded by a nationally known group in the late 50's called the Del Vikings, whose previous songs "Come Go With Me" and "Whispering Bells," had sold over a million copies each. From that, I was able to get a job with a record company promoting records at radio stations and record stores. I was only 18 and living my dream. My job was to make hits of the records our company produced. I was a record promoter.

In late 1963, I came across a group that no one had ever heard of. No radio station wanted to play their music and, consequently, they weren't selling any records. But, I really thought this group was fantastic – they wrote their own songs, played their own instruments and the sound was almost revolutionary. I wanted to make their records a hit and bring them in to town for a concert. Some of their songs I heard back then were "Love Me Do", "She Loves You" and "I Saw Her Standing There". Of course, you know by now we're talking about The Beatles.

When I first talked to a New York agent about bringing The Beatles to the U.S., she also had never heard of them. When she found out they were from England, the agent said, "Forget it, The Beatles will never be big in the U.S., no English rock act has ever gone over well here and never will. They are all too corny." But, I didn't give up. On December 27, 1963, The Beatles released an LP on Capitol Records and the first song on the first side was called "I Want to Hold Your Hand." The rest, as they say, is history.

In 1964, against all odds, I battled the well-established national concert promoters and brought The Beatles to my hometown of Pittsburgh for a sold out concert. I later went on to produce concerts with The Rolling Stones, Led Zeppelin, The Doors, Janis Joplin, Bruce Springsteen, Alice Cooper and just about all the top national entertainers in the world.

As a result, I ultimately became one of the country's biggest concert promoters. It was an amazing experience that I will truly never forget, and I have music to thank for all of it.

*Pat DiCesare*
*Greensburg, Pennsylvania – U.S.A.*
*Author of "Hard Days, Hard Nights"*
*From The Beatles, to The Doors, to The Stones:*
*Insider Stories from a legendary concert promoter*
*www.ConcertPat.com*

## *"There's Always a Song"*

In a nutshell, I learned to play piano by ear when I was around 4 or 5 years old, trying to plunk out songs I heard on the radio, like so many others with an interest in "pop" music. I did take piano lessons with several teachers, but was more interested in improvisation than actual notation. However, my last piano teacher (when I was probably 15 or so) was the real deal. She moved into our small-town neighborhood in Meriden, CT all the way from Austria. She was a very elegant and skilled concert pianist with two grand pianos in her living room. That was very exotic to me, and she lived right across the street too!

She and I would play duets on her pianos and many times just talked about music as much as we played it. In addition to the classics, she introduced me to more modern composers such as Bela Bartok, Aaron Copland, Leonard Bernstein and Igor Stravinsky. Deep stuff, indeed, for a teenager who really just wanted to be in a rock and roll band! But these influences resonated deeply within me, and remain to this day... and for that, I thank the late, great Elly Zimerman. She was one hell of a teacher.

I'm pretty confident that music helps everyone through difficult times. There's always a song, a performance, a simple melody or lyric that touches that special spot; it's a place and emotion so personal, it really can't even be described. For me, the most difficult times have obviously been those when someone close to you passes away. In almost every case, my instant response is to write a song. It's wonderful therapy.

With our band The Hooters, we continue to witness amazing situations every time we play onstage. The audience interactions never cease to excite and inspire us – we can't ask for more than that! And yes, sometimes it works the other way too... seeing a great show can almost be depressing when it has to end. I had the pleasure of seeing Carole King and James Taylor in Philly a few years ago and boy, was I one misty-eyed concert goer. Those classic compositions continue to hold us in their spell and really move us to the core.

And I can remember way back when, hearing Procol Harum's "Whiter Shade Of Pale" on the radio in disbelief. Firstly, what a strange and mysterious song, and exactly why was that a hit? There was no formula for that one, just a compelling and unusual record that captured everyone's ears at the time. And then there's that majestic, haunting, classical organ that became a calling of sorts for me. I'm still trying to get that sound!

I've been very fortunate, where music was always a huge part of my life... listening, learning, writing, recording, and performing. I picked up the basics on piano pretty early on and studied some fundamental classical technique, but it was really all about improvising for me, which led to songwriting and then collaborations in a long string of rock bands. I've been blessed to work with so many wonderful talents throughout my musical journey.

Of course, there were plenty of missteps along the way... that's how you really learn what works. But then, I finally landed some major-label record deals - first, with a group called Baby Grand (two long-lost albums on Arista) and then finally hit on the right combination with The Hooters.

Philadelphia was (and still is) our home base. Our loyal local fans lifted us up and out beyond the city limits to literally seeing and playing around the world. For that, I'm so very thankful. We were lucky (with a lot of perseverance thrown in). And now, there's a long past to cherish and savor, as well as the ever-changing future role that music has in our lives. What a powerful force indeed, with songs that will ring inside our heads forever.

Rock on...!

*Rob Hyman – The Hooters*
*Philadelphia, Pennsylvania – U.S.A.*
*www.RobHyman.com*
*www.HootersMusic.com*

## *"Classical Fab-Four Inspires Some Funky Music"*

I began to be very attracted to and interested in music (and how it was made) as a very small child. Looking back, I can't recall a time in my life when music wasn't on my mind. The first artist to really get to me was Mozart. The simple, yet complex structure of how he wrote (through what I thought was a musical journey that always came back to repeat itself) totally amazed me and drew me in... it inspired me to learn more.

As I grew, I got my first guitar and joined my first band. There were lots of rock and roll influences that came and went along the way, and many that attracted me. But to me, once The Beatles came along, so many new doors were opened. There was a touch of classical music to many of their songs and records. After hearing that, I wanted to know how that music was recorded. In the next phase of my career, I studied the masters like Les Paul, Tom Dowd, Geoff Emerick and many more, to learn about multi track recording.

My quest as a band leader was to build crowds in night clubs. As a teen, I was lucky (at the early age of 15), to be introduced and working with giants in the industry out of the famous Brill Building in Manhattan. I went through many ups and downs along the way, but in 1976, was very fortunate to have written "Play That Funky Music", which has been named one of the top 100 songs of all time. Having been nominated for 2 Grammy's, playing live the night of the Grammy's and actually getting to meet Les Paul, was like my career having gone full circle. We also won the American Music Award, as well as the Billboard "New Band of the Year" for 1976. All in all, music and the business of it, will always be my life.

*Rob Parissi*
*Tampa Bay, Florida – U.S.A.*

## *"What I Did for Love"*

When I was 3 years old, I was always dancing around the house. My mom said "Oh my God, this is our little performer", so she decided to take me to dancing school. The funny thing is, I remember going there and not wanting to dance. I went a couple more times, but cried and still wouldn't dance. About a year and a half later, my pet parakeet died and I was very sad. My mom asked if I wanted another bird, a toy or something. I looked at her and said "I want to go to dancing school". My momma then said "but I took you before and you didn't want to dance". But, I insisted, I really did want to go again. After that, I remember counting the days, hours and minutes until Saturday morning when it was time to go to dance class. By the time I was 7 years old, my dance instructor said to my mother "this girl is going to be a ballerina." I continued my instruction with her, and at the age of 14, I was accepted into the American Ballet Theatre School in New York City and began my career as a ballerina. Once a ballerina, always a ballerina.

I went on to dance with the Royal Ballet of London and was later accepted into The Metropolitan Opera as a ballerina. In addition to singing in opera, there is also dancing and acting involved. After watching many a great opera singer, I one day said to myself "you know what...I want to do that!" With that, I went on to study voice with marvelous teachers and conductors at The Met Opera who took me on at the age of 18. What an education it was for me to learn at The Met! After that, I continued my musical studies at Juilliard. I later went on to the Florida Opera Company and Houston Grand Opera. After a ten year span, I found myself back at The Metropolitan Opera, this time as an opera singer.

I remember the exact moment I realized that I wanted to be an opera singer. It was the "Love Duet" from the opera Madam Butterfly. I was 17 years old when I first heard the powerful emotion in that duet - that was the defining moment for me – that's when I said "I need to be an opera singer". It's a beautiful love story that, sadly, ends in tragedy. That's the standard for operas...there are only a handful of operas in which nobody dies. Madam Butterfly was my eye opener for singing opera, and that combined with being on stage with the greats, was my inspiration. I've been very fortunate to have performed with some of the greatest opera singers in the world, including Luciano Pavarotii and Plácido Domingo. Whenever they were performing, I would just watch in awe, while these amazing artists sang with such power and passion.

A few years ago, my friend Pat Rizzo invited me up to sing at "Vicky's of Santa Fe", a wonderful venue in Indian Wells, California where he often performs. Pat has played with many greats including Sly and Family Stone, Tito Puente, and Frank Sinatra. Whenever I join him on stage I'll usually sing something in the classical/opera vein. However, one night, I decided to sing a jazz number and Pat said "I'm in shock, I've never heard you sing like this!" He then introduced me to Bob Corwin (whose father-in-law was the late great Johnny Mercer). After hearing me sing, Bob said "we've got something here!" So, after years of singing opera and classical, I went into the studio and recorded my first CD, a jazz collection entitled "Simply Rose". I was thrilled when one of my favorite songs from the CD entitled "This is My Life" hit the jazz charts.

Everybody asks "how different is jazz from opera?" It really is not all that different. When you sing opera, it's always in another language and it's all about telling a story...telling the story with passion with emotion. My signature opera role was Richard Strauss's Salome...a wonderful opera, which is very strenuous and musically challenging. For this, I get to dance (as well as sing) and this fascinated me many years ago. I took it on, or it took me on, and it's been a great ride and it's not over. I believe we're all put here for a reason, we're all given a gift...we just need to find that gift and go with what the universe gives you.

Now, I'm going down a new path again and having such fun doing it. For me, singing jazz has been very liberating. In opera, everything is precise...if it's a dotted quarter note, then that's what you sing. However, with jazz and the Great American Songbook, you can do your own interpretation and that's what I'm loving most about it. One of the songs on my CD is the standard "Send in the Clowns". This is a song about an older woman who is a great actress and has been looking for the love of her life. She finally finds it, but he's a much younger man. One night, she's opening this play and her love comes to tell her that he's fallen in love with a younger woman. When you immerse yourself in the story of the song, you do your best to get the emotion across that the writer is feeling. It's very hard to get that drama and passion across in a recording, but that's what we all strive for.

I have had so many amazing experiences in my life through music. I was the first opera singer invited by Bob Hope to be on his Desert Classic show in 1994. I appeared with Bob Hope, Frank Sinatra, John Denver and Vic Damone. It was an incredible lineup and I was so honored to be part of the event. What topped it off for me, was the night of the show; I was supposed to open for Vic Damone and he was watching me rehearse. He came up afterwards and said "Do you mind if I go first? 'Cause I'm not following you!". This was the greatest compliment I ever received. During my career, I also had the opportunity to meet and perform for 3 different US Presidents and got to meet them all (Bill Clinton, George H.W. Bush and Gerald Ford). When you meet the President, it's like you're meeting God, no matter what your affiliation.

I often feel that my life is a lot like "What I Did for Love" from The Chorus Line and it's true. I tell my students, it's one thing to want to be a singer, but you have to be prepared to make a lot of sacrifices along the way. I have a daughter, grandchildren and a wonderful husband who I love very much. But, to be in this business, it's something you have to love just a little bit more. I would honestly wither and die without music. Many of the musicians I'm working with now are in their 80's and 90's and they keep going and going, sharp as a tack...all because they are still involved in music.

*Rose Kingsley*
*Palm Springs, California – U.S.A.*
*www.SimplyRose.info*

## "Million to One"

During my touring days, I had a few dates with Willie Nelson, and one night in particular stands out. We were performing at the Melody Tent in Providence, Rhode Island, and our show happened to be schedule the night after John Kennedy's plane went missing. I mention that, because the entire Kennedy clan was in Providence that weekend for a wedding scheduled the next day. As a result, the entire town was abuzz worrying that another tragedy had befallen this famous family. For us musicians, we wondered if anyone was even going to show for the concert.

As it turned out, we had a full house that night and as the opening act I struggled with what to say about what was happening, if anything at all, during my set. I finally decided to let the music speak and played a song called "Million to One" that talks about the great odds against us in many of life's situations. When I finished the song, I held my fingers crossed up above my head, as a sign that we were all hoping against hope that everything would be alright. The audience completely understood the gesture and the response was deafening.

What makes this even more interesting, is after the show I was approached by a gentleman who politely asked me if the song lyrics were based on a true story. One of the verses tells the tale of a little girl who had gone missing just a few years earlier in small Texas town. After I said they were, he went on to tell me that he was the Sherriff in that Texas town and was currently vacationing in Providence. At that moment, I was completely blown at away at the synchronicity of this revelation in combination with tragedy unfolding that weekend. Truly...the odds and song title "Million to One" were never more appropriate than they were that night.

*Skip Denenberg*
*Philadelphia, Pennsylvania – U.S.A.*
*www.ReverbNation.com/SkipDenenberg*

---

**What can you play with that has no ON switch & no batteries required?**
**A Musical Instrument!**

---

## *"On the Mic"*

I began my entertainment career as a DJ in 1976, but the seeds for my decades behind the mic were planted along ago. My family has a picture of me as a child, just three years old, with headphones on and a microphone in my hand. Even though my uncle taught me the guitar and other musical instruments as I grew older, I was always more interested in playing the records than being the performer. Probably my favorite thing about being a DJ, is getting to meet many of the artists who were the musical heroes of my youth. One of my favorites was always Lee Andrews and the Hearts who had hits in the 50's with songs like "Teardrops" and "Long Lonely Nights". I've now had Lee on my radio show a few times and, like many of my guests, we've become good friends.

*Steve Kurtz – Cruisin' 92.1*
*Clifton Heights, Pennsylvania – U.S.A.*
*www.wvlt.com/SteveKurtz.html*

# *Music*
# *&*
# *Education*

"Hey, who's playing maracas? Nobody in
this band plays maracas."

*Maybe this is why we don't have
maracas in Marching Band.*

## "A Day to Remember at Claremont Elementary"

Assemblies start early at most elementary schools. Kids are having breakfast in the cafeteria, daily announcements are blaring over a crackly loudspeaker, custodians are cleaning the floor in front of the stage and musicians are setting up sound equipment. On this day, we were setting up to perform our show entitled "Dare to be Writer's".

Typically, curiosity overwhelms a few students who break away from their breakfast table and come to the edge of the stage with big eyes and ask: "What is this?", "Is everybody coming?", "Can I come on stage?". At Claremont Elementary, we were very pleased to be able to say "Yes, everyone is coming". It may seem strange now to think that anyone might be excluded. At that time, Special Education classes were sometimes not included in assemblies, for fear that they might disrupt the performance.

The Claremont kids were a great crowd as we weaved together many examples of different styles of music and writing. We performed songs that can make you laugh, learn things, be silly and also make you think. One particular song called "Rachel", which was part of the older kid's performance, focused on special needs kids from their perspective. It was delicate to perform this song with special needs kids in the audience, but the mood of the room was right and we decided to go for it with all the sincerity we could muster. It worked! AND it was magical! The Special Ed teacher stood up and held one of her prize students up for all to see and acknowledge. Her student smiled with such pride.

Music, does indeed, matter. It brings us together as a community and helps us express emotions that are sometimes hard to say. Many children do not have the opportunity to experience live theater, unless it happens at their school.  Teachers and students work hard and they need their spirits lifted and their routines altered, now and then, to refresh their motivation.  We sincerely hope school assemblies will always continue to cement the powerful relationship between music and education.

*Laura and Tim Battersby - "The Battersbys"*
*Tampa, Florida – U.S.A.*
*The BatDuo, Grammy Nominees*
*www.BattersbyDuo.com*

## "Keep Your Ears Open"

When I was growing up, I was a nerd. In fact, I was the definition of a nerd. Being the walking nerd checklist that I was - glasses, too skinny, greasy hair, no social skills - I was easy prey for the animals in the elementary and middle school hallways. The thing about being a nerd is, you are put down so often that after a while, you start to believe it. You need something in your life that will help you believe in yourself, something you are good at, which can be recognized by the other kids your age.  Not respected mind you, but maybe you'll get punched in the stomach a little less often.

In fifth grade, I started playing the trumpet and something happened. I was still a nerd, but I found out that I could do something. Not only could I do it, but I was actually pretty good at it.  And in sixth grade, I got the first public recognition of my life. The middle school band was to perform at the high school band festival and receive a participation trophy. The band members got to vote on which one of us would go out and receive that trophy. Everyone voted and picked me.  ME!  They weren't my friends, in fact some of them were still punching me in the locker room, but I was finally *recognized*.

Looking back, it might have been the break I needed. I believed in my ability to make music, how it made me feel and what it could do for me. Decades later, I find myself in the position to recognize kids for what they are doing. Sometimes, all a kid needs is a break. In a world where academic or athletic success (or even mediocrity) is celebrated, I can give a kid the break they might need in their lives through music. Whenever I do that, I know exactly what it means to them. For you see, I was that kid.

I grew up listening to my dad and uncle play the guitar, banjo and sing in the basement of my house. They would drink beer, smoke cigars and harmonize (sometimes well) to Peter, Paul and Mary or The Beach Boys or to groups I was too young to recognize. My cousin and I would sit in my room and make fun of them. We would laugh, imitate them and howl like dogs. What I didn't know at the time, was that when my dad and uncle were younger, they would bring their instruments to parties, play all night and impress the ladies. A lot more than my cousin and I were accomplishing. With no formal training, just a love of music and a lot of practice, I watched my dad gain fulfillment from singing and playing guitar. I can only assume that part of my determination to complete a degree in music and teach as a professional came from this early insight into music's power.

When I think about how music has affected my life, it reads almost like a checklist:

- the Discipline of Music has taught me to be timely, organized, goal-oriented and given me a work ethic.

- the Science of Music has given me problem solving skills and a connection to math and physics that I never had.

- the Art of Music has allowed me to get in touch with my inner expression and appreciate the expression of others.

- the Physicality of Music has taught me the importance of diet and exercise and given me physical strength and endurance.

- the Spirituality of Music has given me priceless moments, brought me in touch with my soul and the souls of others.

If I could offer just one piece of advice to future musicians, music educators and music lovers all around the world, it would be to "keep your ears open"! Strive to be nonjudgmental, thoughtful and try to fully utilize your listening skills - just like the kind your music teacher tried to get you to do.  By doing this, you can quite literally become a force to change the world.

*Craig Snyder*
*Media, Pennsylvania – U.S.A.*
*Director of Bands - Penncrest High School*
*Trumpet Player, Conductor & Clinician*
*Proud Former & Current Nerd*
*www.PenncrestBand.org*

## *"Dorothy Cho – Warrior of Hope"*

"Mummy, does she read in print or Braille?" a sweet nine year old Dorothy whispers to her mom in Korean. That is how this blind little girl distinguishes whether a person is sighted or not. Since Dorothy has never been able to see with her eyes, she absorbs the world through sounds, smells and touch. The sighted can never imagine how astoundingly beautiful her world is. "Can I feel your hair, Ms. Khim?", Dorothy asks me when we first met.

"Certainly, sweetie", I answered and felt the tingly sensation of her fingers running through my hair. "You have very pretty, smooth and straight hair, it's just like mine", Dorothy remarked. I have been reeled into Dorothy's magical world ever since and have the incredible pleasure of being her ukulele teacher at the Academy of Music for the Blind, the only blind music school in America that offers a comprehensive music education dedicated to blind children.

Dorothy is amongst a handful of blessed children who benefited from early intervention tactile and sensory learning at the Blind Children's Learning Center (BCLC) in Orange County, California before she was two years old. Growing up, her parents were determined to give her the best education available to blind children. They courageously uprooted from Korea in order to pursue this hope, despite not knowing anyone here in America or much English. Dorothy flourished at BCLC and saw her world through a cornucopia of textures, shapes and sounds. Most importantly, Dorothy saw music clearly from an early age. At the same time she began learning how to speak, she sang her first tune of Jingle Bells. "Dorothy sings more than she speaks throughout her day", Dorothy's mom would tell us. Since there were not many visual toys that Dorothy could play with, her parents tried to introduce her to some musical instruments, however, she was afraid to touch them. They were not sure what this phobia was about and how to overcome it.

Thankfully, at seven years of age, Dorothy met an influential visually impaired Vocational Instruction teacher who introduced her to the guitar. She was so fascinated with the sounds and vibrations of the string, that she refused to put her guitar down, even when it was bedtime. She had not learned to play it yet and, once again, her parents were on a mission to find the right teacher for Dorothy. They were sure that Dorothy loved music, and if she was taught by a music teacher who specialized in teaching blind children, she would learn very quickly.

Another milestone in Dorothy's musical journey occurred when she joined the Johnny Mercer Choir offered by the Braille Institute. It was here that her parents truly discovered her gift in singing. She shone in the presence of other blind choir members and looked forward to every practice and performance. She was always full of energy whenever given the opportunity to sing. They continued to see Dorothy sing like an angel, and before long, she was given the opportunity to perform the national Anthem for the Anaheim Ducks game and a special event at the Curtis Theater. Each time Dorothy performed, her parents would experience the audience gasping in awe, as their hearts were touched by Dorothy's beautiful voice.

When Dorothy was eight years old, her parents miraculously discovered the Academy of Music for the Blind (AMB). Dorothy auditioned with the Director, David Pinto, and was immediately enrolled. Over the next month, Dorothy's instrumental abilities propelled forward and amazingly, her fear of musical instruments completely disappeared. On the contrary, her fingers now moved fluidly on different instruments with David Pinto's guidance. Mr. Pinto has been teaching blind musicians for over twenty years and developed an effective method that brings the best out of the students, optimizing their incredible focus, immaculate pitch and heightened sensory motor skills. He started this non-profit school ten years ago with the vision to empower children ages 4-19 with music. He believes that these talented blind students deserve the same music education available to sighted students. At this very special school, Dorothy not only excelled in music, but also found a sense of belonging with her peers who were blind, just like her. In her own words, "I found a few BFF's here at AMB and I love going on play dates with them". She has since started public school at Claire Barton's Elementary, where she is among just three blind students in the entire school and the only blind student in her grade.

AMB is held every Saturday at the Junior Blind of America campus in Los Angeles. Her Mom claims that Dorothy's self-esteem and confidence was boosted when she began making friends in this loving and supportive network of families bound together by the same passion for music and condition of blindness. It made her want to practice harder and improve her musical talents. Every Saturday, she is given the opportunity to hone her performance skills in front of an audience during Sharetime. AMB instills not only the love of music, but an avenue that our students can contribute to the world through their musical abilities. Dorothy has mastered Braille Music and TypeAbility, a special interactive computer program that sharpens blind student's typing skills so they can navigate around adaptive computers easily. AMB also offers a unique sound engineering class using special software created to help blind musicians compose and record their own music independently.

I asked Dorothy what she wanted to be when she grew up, and she answered with a smile, "I want to be a singer and make a mark in the world with my music". We are confident that when you experience Dorothy's singing, your heart will be touched by her seemingly magical voice. She is a warrior of hope to all children in this world, blind or sighted, to rise above their adversities and pursue their dreams.

*Khim Teoh – Academy of Music for the Blind*
*Los Angeles, California – U.S.A.*
*www.OurAMB.org*
*www.DorothyCho.com*

## *"HOME"*

"Oh, I miss the comfort of this house..." This is a line from the song "Lakehouse" by the band Of Monsters and Men. I used to perform this song with my band HOME and this line epitomizes how I feel looking back at the experiences I had with my middle school band.

In the basement of a small school in the middle of South Philadelphia, something life changing was created. In the third grade, we were informed that the school had gotten a new music teacher Mr. Argerakis, or "Mr. A", for short. During this time, my life was not good. What's funny, is I didn't even know why I felt this way and that made it even worse. Starting before I was in middle school, I always felt a sense of sadness. But, I was always interested in music, and when I first stepped into the music room at Andrew Jackson School, it made the sadness go away for an hour or so.

Later that school year, I found out that Mr. A was starting a band. I was so excited! I always wanted to play the piano and sing and I knew that this was my chance. My older sister, Joycelyn, and my younger sister, Julia, were interested as well. I knew Julia (who was in the second grade) and I (third grade) were too young to join, but Joycelyn was not. She joined the first band and ended up becoming captain. I was extremely proud of her and a bit jealous. I would go to every single rehearsal and sit, either behind the drums where no one could see me or next to the piano player, and try to figure out the chords. Mr. A would often tell me to grab a guitar and play along, but I felt too intimidated by the older students.

When I got to sixth grade, Mr. A started a 'Junior band' as a way to nurture younger talent. It was basically all the 6th and 7th graders in the "Jr." band and the 8th graders, including Joycelyn, in the 'Senior band'. Of course, I joined the junior band. For the first rehearsal, I played guitar, but

Mr. A and I both knew that I was dying to be in the piano chair. The band brought together kids of many different cultures, with whom I quickly bonded. I made a lot of new friends and, most importantly, I didn't feel as bad as before. In the first year, the Junior band struggled a lot. Looking back, the struggles and hard work were a real bonding experience, especially for the kids who stuck together. Amazingly, I got the position of being captain. That year, our only performances were as an opening act for the senior band. Little did I know how much we were going to thrive the following year.

The "Senior" band graduated in June of 2013, and the following September I was now in the main band. At this time, I was just starting the 7th grade. For the first few months, we played relatively easy songs like Ben E. King's, "Stand By Me", Sam Cooke's, "Cupid" and Coldplay's, "Yellow". These were songs that were an ideal match for our musical skills at the time. After winter break, however, something sparked in us. We came back full of energy and began working on more challenging songs like Bon Jovi's, "Livin' On A Prayer", Of Monsters and Men's, "Little Talks" and many others. By springtime, our set list had grown to over twenty songs!

Before the winter break, we had decided to try and name the band. Countless suggestions were discussed, but nothing seemed to stick. Nothing defined who we were becoming as a band. I suddenly had an idea! With much apprehension, I went to Mr. A and said, "Mr. A, we spend so much time in the music room, we're here before school, during school, after school and, sometimes, even on weekends. We're all so close that it feels like family...like a home. So, I suggest we call the band, "HOME"." Mr. A, without hesitation, said "that's it!" and we have been known as HOME ever since.

Over the course of the next two years, we gigged regularly, including performances at the annual Christmas

Tree lighting ceremony in South Philadelphia, the Wilma Theater, World Café Live, and a Musicopia event at Citizens Bank Ballpark where we were joined on-stage by the Phillies Phanatic! We played The Vie Ballroom on Broad Street, the Atlantic City Convention Center and even Philadelphia's historic Trocadero Theater, where we were joined on stage by the Hooters' David Uosikkinen, Jay Z's trumpeter, Matt Cappy, and Rock and Roll Hall of Famer, Garth Hudson! We were also mentored by Josh Groban, who invited us to his concert at the Wells Fargo center, brought us backstage and spoke about us in front of 15,000 people! We were visited by Rob Hyman, founding member of The Hooter's, who also co-wrote Cyndi Lauper's, "Time After Time. We got to perform "Time After Time" with Rob, as well as the songs "Satellite" and "All You Zombies" by the Hooters.

During this time, I even gave a keynote speech, along with Mr. A, at The University of Pennsylvania about the importance of HOME in my life and the importance of music in public education. I also gave a speech to the entire student body of The Shipley School in Bryn Mawr, Pennsylvania during one of our many performances there.

The pinnacle of our "career" came when the President of the American Federation of Teachers, Randi Weingarten, invited us to play at the AFT National Convention in Washington D.C. on July 22, 2013. We were treated like kings and queens, staying in beautiful hotel rooms, eating fancy dinners, rode in a huge "tour" bus and of course, we got to perform in front of thousands! Filmmaker, George Silvertooth made a documentary about us during this time, telling our story, the struggles we faced and our "road to Washington". We've also been featured in articles on WXPN.org and the front page of the Philadelphia Inquirer!

As I neared the end of 8$^{th}$ grade, the sadness began to creep in my mind again, as I felt this amazing chapter of my life slowly coming to an end. This time, the feeling was worse than ever before. Going through an outpatient hospital and undergoing therapy helped a lot, but one of the main reasons for my recovery from a lifetime struggle of depression, was my band and Mr. A. Learning, practicing and performing music made me extremely happy and kept me going. It still does.

Recently, in the Spring of 2015, our band HOME was reunited when we had the opportunity to meet our favorite band, Of Monsters and Men! It all started with me sending a few videos to their manager the previous year. The band had seen videos of us performing several of their songs and loved it. Unfortunately, they could not visit us at the time. But, when I found out they were on tour again, Mr. A and I emailed them once again. They said they would love to come see us. Within a month or so, I was sitting next to them, playing their songs WITH them! I couldn't believe it. I can't thank HOME and Mr. A enough for enabling me to meet my favorite band, who came all the way from Iceland! Even after my middle school years are over, I am so blessed to still be a part of HOME!

Now, I am a student at the top high school in Philadelphia, Central H.S. Whenever I crave music, Mr. A always welcomes me with open arms...and it's only a subway ride away. Part of the initial concept of HOME, was that the door would always be open for alumni to come back and sit in with the current band; you can come back to Andrew Jackson and see kids from years past...back in the room jamming or just seeing what the current version of HOME is up to. Without music, my band, and Mr. A, I honestly don't know where my life would be. I'm forever grateful for this amazing experience.

*"And if I had the choice, Yeah, I'd always wanna be there. Those were the best days of my life"* - Bryan Adams

*Jasmine Mya Yedra*
*Philadelphia, Pennsylvania – U.S.A.*

## *"Keep Music Alive"*

I am a music educator in Central Illinois and St. Louis, Missouri, and music has been a part of my life since childhood. My parents, grandparents, aunts, uncles, and cousins (on both sides of my family) actively sang and played instruments around the house, at family gatherings, and in church services. I began taking piano lessons in third grade and added clarinet in fifth grade, when I started band. I continued on in the school music program through my senior year of high school (2004). All of these experiences added to my skill development, not just in music, but in coordination, problem solving, mathematics, physics, history, language, and many other areas of education and life enrichment.

By the time I finished my Bachelor's in Music Education in 2010, I realized how much the public school music education system was failing due to lack of support, funds, and time to devote to the success of the program. This really resonated with me when my hometown removed fifth grade band from the elementary schools. I immediately thought, "They should be starting a year earlier, not later!" The earlier a person begins their involvement in music, the more beneficial and long-lasting the results will be. It was at that point that I decided to be proactive in the preservation of music education for future generations. In 2013, I established Notes and Rhythms: School of Fine Arts in my community and currently provide music lessons to local students with the hope of expanding to cover all of the arts.

I have recently returned to school to earn a degree in Music Therapy, a field which further illustrates the importance of music in everyone's lives. Evidence of the effects music has on our mind and body is all around us! Think about your own experiences. Do you have a favorite song? Why is it your favorite? Chances are, it reminds you of something or someone or speaks to you in some very special way. Music is a super power that connects the brain to life events through memory and emotions. Do you listen to music when you exercise? Why? Most likely because the music you choose motivates you to move and you probably find yourself moving in time with the selected song. These are just a few of the countless examples of how music benefits the human body on a daily basis.

For years, I have expressed the value of music education in every person's life and I firmly believe in all of the benefits music encompasses. Can you imagine your life without music? Ask yourself this question, the next time you hear of a community losing any aspect of music education or if you are faced with the decision to vote for or against keeping music in your schools.

*Marcy Holub*
*Jerseyville, Illinois – U.S.A.*
*Notes & Rhythms*
*www.NotesAndRhythms.com*

---

**If kids think they are "playing" music instead of "practicing" music, they'll want to PLAY more!**

## "How Marching Band Changed My Life at Age 40!"

I was never very involved in high school. I didn't play sports and I wasn't in any clubs. The final bell rang at 2:40pm - if I wasn't already a mile down the road by 2:45, it was because I was serving detention. For me, "being involved" equated to conforming, or giving in, or... something. What it was I would have been giving in to, I have no idea now and I'm not sure I knew back then.

I'm married now, with two teenage children. Both of them are hopeless band nerds, and believe me when I say, there is no way for me to fully express the unabashed pride and affection I feel when I make that statement.

But, I didn't always feel that way. Band, especially marching band, is an enormous time commitment for students and their parents too. The rehearsal schedule is filled with long, grueling, twelve-hour days spent on a blacktop in 90+ degree weather. Most days, rehearsals run even longer than scheduled. Competitions can often result in the band not arriving back home until 3 or 4 in the morning.

For parents, having a kid in marching band can be inconvenient and annoying. It can make or break weekend plans and even cancel vacations. For a guy like me, the whole program, initially, seemed ridiculous and way too much.

Now, I want to be clear: When I say my kids are hopeless band nerds, I'm not saying that marching band is a hobby they enjoy, not even close. They love marching band with an unquenchable passion, and it was that way from their first day of rookie band camp. So, even in the beginning, it was hard for me to speak out against it...as much I may have wanted to.

During my daughter's first year with the band, I didn't really pay a lot of attention. I worked a lot - night hours, which are a staple when you own a pizzeria - and my wife handled most of the picking-up and dropping-off duties. Honestly, I didn't think my daughter would stick with it, but she did. It became so important to her that when her second year rolled around, I agreed to begin fundraising for the band through my pizzeria. As a result, I began spending some time at the school.

Let me tell you - I was blown away, completely and immediately. It could be 8:00 pm and there would still be 200+ kids at the school, still working hard. And they were happy to be there! My wife scoffs every time I say it, but I still can't help marveling at the idea that there is a whole other world, a 'school after school', that I never knew existed.

I began coming early to pick up my daughter (and eventually my son too, who joined during middle school), just so I could watch them rehearse. I marveled at their attention to detail, their unrelenting spirit, and the pride with which they carried themselves. Even after 12 hours in the hot sun, they still gave it their all and loved every minute of it.

My son and daughter both look so alive, so proud, especially during performances - something that would have terrified me when I was in high school. This made me realize there was a major component in my own life that was missing, one that had never been there before, simply because I never had the courage to commit to doing something I love. Work and money had always seemed too important - an excuse. But, there my kids were, doing both what they had to do (regular school, academics) as well what they loved. They'd committed. Fearlessly.

And so, in November of 2011, I wrote the opening line to my first novel. It wasn't ready for publication until April of 2013...work kept getting in the way, family and friends kept getting in the way, life kept getting in the way, but I stuck with it. I stayed committed. If my kids could do it, I could do it!

That novel has now found its way onto more than 50,000 e-readers. My next four novels have already sold thousands of copies. I get fan mail. I have an enormous subscriber list that gets bigger every day.

Courage, conviction and commitment to a passion were all it took, and I never would have learned that lesson if not for my kids and, of all things, high school marching band...at age 40.

*Matthew Keith*
*Vine Grove, Kentucky – U.S.A.*
*www.MatthewKeith.net*
*Author of the Young Adult SciFi Series "Watchers of the Night"*

## *"I Teach People, Not Pianos"*

Once, when I went golfing as a single, I was asked by the gentleman with whom I had been paired, what I did for a living. I replied, "I'm an educator." He continued, "What do you teach?" Feeling a bit spunky, I said, "People." He chuckled and further questioned, "What subject?" I responded, "Music." "Oh, what instrument?" he asked. "Piano." "Oh, so you're a piano teacher," was his final comment.

"No," I continued. "Saying I'm a 'piano teacher' implies that I teach pianos, Pianos are perfectly fine being pianos without my assistance. I assist people in growing as people, through the language of music, at the piano."

I am so fortunate, as a music teacher, to have the incredible opportunity to impact a child, not just as a developing musician, but more importantly as a developing person. This is because the study of an instrument puts us up against learning challenges that have little to do with music, and much more to do with how each of us learn. I have the unique privilege to provide my students with skills that will enable them to achieve all that they desire, both musically and personally.

Through the study of music, we have the opportunity to provide our students with the problem solving skills that will enable them to achieve anything. They must learn how to handle frustration - what better time than when they are young, since frustration is an inevitable part of the human learning experience? They must learn how to create consistent goals that enable them to experience the feeling of fulfillment and pride, which are the ultimate motivators. Greater than any external trophies, these internal rewards of fulfillment and pride have the ability to propel our students to great levels of success. They must learn how to manage their own negative self-talk. We have the amazing opportunity to show them how.

Once they believe in themselves, a student will fulfill their greatest potential; not just as a musician, but as a person.

*Nick Ambrosino*
*Nesconset, New York – U.S.A.*
*Learning Specialist, Author & Speaker*
*Author of "Coffee with Ray" & "Lessons with Matt"*
*www.NickAmbrosino.com*
*www.MusicSimplyMusic.com*

## *"A Hidden Star"*

I am a singer-songwriter specializing in educational music for elementary school-aged children. Over the last 29 years, I have performed in hundreds of schools throughout the US with my husband accompanying me on guitar and bass, and sometimes with a drummer.

One day, a few years ago, we performed for third graders at a school in a suburb of Boston, MA. They wanted my Character show, which is one of my 18 different programs. Teachers and students were seated on the floor in front of us; we were on a stage only a few steps up from floor level.

All my shows are highly interactive, with every song involving audience participation. Sometimes they are participating from their seats; sometimes I ask for volunteers to come join us on stage. On this particular day, I asked for two children to volunteer to come up to sing some solo parts. For this, I needed kids who were not shy and who felt comfortable and confident to sing by themselves. Hands shot up; as is my wont, I also asked the audience to point to someone they thought would do a good job. Many children excitedly pointed to one particular boy whose hand was up. I picked him, along with a girl, who was similarly selected by her classmates.

Suddenly I saw a teacher waving her arms wildly, indicating "NOT THAT BOY!" but it was too late; he was already on his way to the stage. I did not know why that teacher wanted this boy "unpicked," so I just let him come up onstage. The teacher jumped up from where she had been sitting and perched right on the steps below the boy, obviously to keep an eye on him. "Uh oh," I thought, "am I in for some trouble? Is this kid a class clown or will he sabotage the show somehow? What???" Those of us who perform regularly for children have learned to be prepared for *anything.*

I proceeded to give the two kids their instructions, which were simple; they just needed to echo the lines that I sang to them, right after me. Each held a microphone; neither seemed particularly nervous about singing a solo on a song they had never heard before.

We launched into the song and when it came time for the girl to "be my echo" she did a beautiful job and all the third graders cheered and applauded. Then it was the boy's turn...

I still did not know what the problem was, but in any case it was too late to do anything about it. Being a veteran of thousands of shows throughout the decades, I figured I'd seen it all and could handle whatever happened. When it came time for the boy to echo my lines, he did a SUPER job. I didn't know what the big deal with the teacher was; it all seemed routine and just fine. At the end of his part, the entire room erupted into cheers, applause, whistles and hoots. When the song ended, I had the two volunteers take a bow and asked the audience to give them a big hand...the response was deafening. The teacher sitting on the stage steps looked relieved.

After the show, I approached the teacher who had tried to stop the boy to ask what the situation was. As it turns out, this boy was autistic and barely spoke a word in school. He had difficulty with every task and was socially isolated. I asked her if the kids who "volunteered" him were trying to be kind and helpful in getting him picked, or were they *teasing* him, thinking he would fail in front of the whole audience? She said she felt they were picking on him and laughing about it, pointing to him for whatever mean reasons they had. She had gone up and sat at his feet in order to help him succeed; but it turned out he needed no help at all.

When this boy opened his mouth, he followed my instructions perfectly AND had a lovely voice! He showed everyone what he was capable of. As he descended triumphantly from the stage, the cheers, high-fives and back slaps his schoolmates gave him showed their newfound respect for this little boy. After I heard the explanation as we were getting ready to pack up I felt close to tears. This was one of the most memorable shows we've ever experienced. I know it changed my life, and I hope it changed a few others' in that school as well, especially that little boy's.

*Patricia Shih*
*Huntington, New York – U.S.A.*
*www.PatriciaShih.com*
*www.PatriciaShihArt.com*
*www.UndocumentedDoc.com*
*www.TrulyRottenGigsFromHell.com*

---

## One surefire way to help change the world for the better is to Teach Music.

---

### *"An Open Letter to All School Superintendents"*

Dear American Educators,

I am writing to voice my support for comprehensive arts education in our public schools. The arts are vital to our lives and our nation and the reasons why are seemingly endless. Visual arts, music, theater, dance, creative writing, handicrafts, and other forms of creative expression enrich our lives. The arts also enlighten us as people and add vibrancy and dynamics to our society. To understand and appreciate the arts is to understand and appreciate our culture. Poetry, painting, music and other art forms are important, because they are a reflection of the lives we lead.

For example: Knowing the arts is key to understanding our country's history and what makes America "America". This is especially true of creative writing and music, which tell stories that get passed from one generation to the next. A prime example of this is "The Star Spangled Banner" by Francis Scott Key. Not only is it our national anthem, but it is also a living document and testimonial about a pivotal piece of American history and the resolve of the American people.

Investment in arts education benefits far more people than just visual art and music students. Studies have proven that professional fields, of all types, benefit by students receiving a well-rounded education. The arts excel in teaching innovation, context and excellence; learning the arts also strengthens a person's ability to think critically and "outside the box." Our future doctors, nurses, scientists, engineers and more all benefit from arts education. When children learn to draw, they are helping to develop their fine eye-hand coordination. Learning to play a musical instrument at a young age aids the development of a child's cognitive function. Additional research reveals a strong link between music and visual arts education and higher achievement, both academically and well into adulthood. The arts also teach how collaboration and independent thought work together and how to create original ideas that fit within existing frameworks, abilities that are vital in today's technological world.

Investment in the arts generates billions of dollars in economic activity, which translates directly into jobs and influence, both at home and around the globe. America's top export is not technology, automotive, agriculture or weapons. It's music, book publishing, cinematography and fine arts. There is a global market for what America creates, and the arts are a key component contributing to our country's status in the world.

As Americans, we should realize this better than anyone. It is America that created the concepts of free markets and mass distribution, which empowers creators and entrepreneurs by rewarding them. It is America that created the worldwide distribution framework that delivers information and entertainment to a global audience. We created the Walt Disney's and the Warner Brothers of the world, the tastemakers of art as entertainment. The film and TV studios of Hollywood are billion dollar enterprises, selling fantasy and adventure to an eager audience worldwide. Visual artists, such as Norman Rockwell and Andrew Wyeth, are known throughout the world; their works serving as a window into American life. And it was America who created the modern record company that has provided the soundtrack to our lives. All of these businesses need an educated workforce and one with an education that includes the arts.

Despite all the evidence of the benefits that comprehensive arts education provides our youngsters and society, there are still some who fail to understand the need for the arts as part of our public school curricula. A few are even outright hostile to the arts, both in school and the community at large. As America loses its competitive edge and its world status begins to diminish, I find their opposition quite disturbing. The role of the arts in society is of no less consequence than the roles of industry, science, health care or banking.

Visual arts, music, cinema, radio/TV, book publishing and other art forms create jobs and fills our tax coffers, all the while promoting international good will and enriching our cultural identity and understanding. It's time that those with an axe to grind stop using public school arts programs as political chess pieces. By refusing to invest in arts education, we are in danger of creating a culturally stagnant society. We risk robbing our communities of what makes them vibrant and unique, and creating disincentives towards investing in both our young people and our businesses here at home. And history will judge us harshly for it.

Now think about what our lives would be like without our great American musicians, poets, visual artists and architects. How about our writers, photographers, filmmakers, and actors? Our country would lose its edge in more ways than we can possibly imagine. These are just a few of the many reasons why I encourage you to support music and art education in our public schools.

*Peter P. Carli II*
*Goldsboro/Etters, Pennsylvania – U.S.A.*
*www.RadiationRoom.com*

# *Music*
# *&*
# *Healing*

"Tommy is in the other room playing
with the triangle we bought him in
Bermuda."

*Rumor has it some musical instruments
are more magical than others.*

## "The Jazz Sanctuary"

In December of 2006, I suffered a Brain AVM, otherwise known as an arteriovenous malformation. After 13 hours of surgery, 33 days of recuperation in Jefferson Hospital, and aided by the unflinching support of my wife, my friends and prayers of priests and parishioners, I was finally on the mend.

Afterwards, I played the bass five to six hours a day for a year, attempting to regain my hand-eye coordination and the ability to read once again. It was during that time, that I decided to give back to those who had supported me through that difficult time. And so, The Jazz Sanctuary was born, along with the Jazz & Joe concerts. We provide music events, free of charge, Sunday through Thursday for any non-profit organization. Over the last 5 years, we have supplied music for over 250 events. I have served without remuneration, of any kind, as my way of giving back. I am grateful each day and love the joy of music we bring to people through our programs every week.

*Alan Segal*
*Philadelphia, Pennsylvania – U.S.A.*
*Executive Director – The Jazz Sanctuary*
*www.TheJazzSanctuary.com*

## "I Truly Could Not Live a Day"

I have always loved all kinds of music! Music held me together when my son's heart stopped and I had to do CPR. I kept a steady song running through my head for the beats & breaths. Then, while he was on life support, I would take breaks and listen to a tune or two and then go back to the room after I had gathered myself together. Two years later, when my husband was critically ill and in the hospital for 14 months, music is once again what kept me going. I listened to it constantly in the car, going back & forth from the hospital. I'd sit in the hospital and sing songs in my head as I sat there 12 to 16 hours a day. Every time we thought he was getting better, another crisis would try to take him away.

Whenever the times were tough in my life, the songs in my heart made me stronger. Now, when I am upset, I turn on the radio and dance my cares away. Dancing and music releases the tensions and redeems my soul. Music is the best gift God has given us. It makes even the most unbearable times easier to cope with. The fact is, music expresses that which cannot be put into words and that which cannot remain silent. Music comes from within and helps release all the pain, sorrow, stress and worries in our lives and the result is pure happiness. I truly could not live a day without music!

*Ann Kelly*
*Delaware County, PA - U.S.A.*

**Music connects our hearts with humanity.**

## *"The Living Years"*

When my father passed away, I wasn't all together "getting it", until I happened to be driving and heard the Mike and The Mechanics' song, "The Living Years". It reached deep inside of me and broke it all loose. Nothing could have done that like a song. First of all, Mike Rutherford's words are brilliant and very real. Second, the singer, Paul Carrack, brought it home beautifully. This song helped my heart like nothing else could.

*Bill Champlin*
*www.BillChamplin.com*
*www.Facebook.com/BillChamplinMusic*
*www.SonsOfChamplin.com*
*www.Facebook.com/SonsOfChamplin*

## *"Music Will Never Give Up on Us"*

When I look back at the terrible place I was in, and compare it to the perfect life I have now, I know it was music that led me here and saved me from my addiction. If I tell you music is also responsible for connecting me with my wife, and thus the birth of my son, you'd probably think I was over exaggerating; believe me when I tell you, I'm not. My son owes his existence in this life to music, just as I owe my own life to music.

Some years ago, I made the awful decision to date a girl who was a heroin addict. One thing led to another and the next thing I knew, I was a full blown junkie. It got so bad, that I actually started to sell my most treasured possessions; my instruments and recording gear. I managed to keep just one acoustic guitar, but that was only because it was such a piece of crap that no one would buy it. I did try...even though it broke my heart to even think of not having at least one guitar. But, the drive of a heroin addict's desire to not go through opiate withdrawal is unimaginably more powerful than the human conscience on its best day.

So, I continued to write music and play coffee house type gigs with my piece of garbage acoustic guitar, all the while promising myself, day after day, that "I would get clean tomorrow" and start buying new gear with the money I would save from not having to buy dope. That tomorrow took 3 or 4 years and countless hours of misery and hopelessness, to finally come. I remember sitting in my car in the middle of Trenton, New Jersey...waiting for my dealer to show up. I'd listen to certain songs that would almost inspire me to be stronger and drive away from the prison I kept myself in, but that feeling would inevitably fade, as the songs did.

What finally gave me the will power to stay strong and fight through the addiction, was my intense desire to record the huge library of songs I had been writing. My computer was filled with well over 200 song ideas that I would record into the computer's microphone anytime I had a catchy riff or vocal melody. This has since evolved into using my smartphone and a recording app, but that routine was started way back when I still had a pager. The unfinished song ideas I had compiled over the years were sitting and collecting dust inside my old computer tower. It was driving me crazy that such good material would never see the light of day. So I finally got clean, got a lousy job in a manufacturing plant and toughed out the years; all the while building my gear collection back to its former glory and well beyond. I now have a fully equipped pro grade recording studio and I'm still chipping away at those 200 song ideas, giving them their due justice with the best quality they can be recorded with. Around a year after I cleaned myself up, I began recording again with some basic gear I acquired. I eventually decided to put some of the songs up on Myspace under the band name 'The Nine Aligned'. For those of you kids who have no idea what Myspace is, picture Facebook with a lot less comments popping up from your friends. My wife, who was only a random music fan at that time, was browsing around and searching for some songs by Nine Inch Nails on their Myspace page. She typed their band name into the search box and my band 'The Nine Aligned' came up instead. After clicking through she discovered that she liked my music enough to send me a private message. She wrote asking why I hardly had any Myspace friends, as she felt my music was as good as any mainstream band. I replied back and we continued to write each other for 3 years. One day, we finally called each other and eventually decided to meet in person. I was in Pennsylvania and she lived in North Carolina, so it was a big step for both of us. But, we took the chance and have been together ever since.

So, as you can see, there really isn't anything in my life that I don't, in some way, owe to music. Whether we realize it or not, everyone needs music, even if many will never understand what music does for their lives. The truth is, music will never give up on us, even if our backs stay forever turned to it. I, for one, will never forget what music has done for me.

*Chris McDermott*
*Philadelphia, Pennsylvania – U.S.A.*
*www.EveOfRelease.com*

## "A Whisper Heard Around The World"

I spent a lot of time with my grandmother Ruthye, and as a result was EXTREMELY close to her. She was a great story-teller and a wonderful cook. Her husband, my grandfather, was a career military man. So, much of her life was spent travelling around the world with him. She was an avid supporter of the military and would often tell me stories about her adventures and how she would cook big meals for all the military people that were away from their families. I loved hearing her tales and how she made everyone feel special, especially me.

When my grandmother was first diagnosed with cancer, I was in denial of how serious it was. When she died not long after her diagnosis, I was emotionally crushed. One night, following her death, I was writing songs for my first album. A song called "Whisper" spilled out of me. It's a song about missing someone terribly. It's rare for me to consider a song finished in one night, but this was the case with "Whisper". When I realized that the song also touched on the emotions that military families (wives, children, parents and friends) feel when someone special is away serving in the military, I made a music video of the song to reflect that.

Although I was only 11 years old when I wrote and recorded this song, the video has been viewed on YouTube by people in over 149 different countries. I've received thousands of comments, emails and messages from people of all ages, races, and religions, stating how "Whisper" touched them and helped ease their pain. Since the song was released in 2012, I have donated all of the proceeds from online sales to the USO (United Service Organization) in honor of my grandmother's lifelong dedication to the military. The USO is a nonprofit, non-government agency that provides support programs and services designed to meet the ever-changing needs of troops and their families.

It's humbling to think that I could touch so many people with a song that I wrote at such a young age. The truth is, it may not have happened without the dedication and encouragement from my elementary school music teacher Mr. Tracy Morris and Principal Jill Leinhauser, at Jacksonville Beach Elementary. Not only did their promotion of the arts in schools inspire me to want to get involved, their support helped me get over severe stage fright. Without them, I might not have the career in music I have today; and without it, the opportunity to touch all of the people my music has reached.

*Dalton Cyr*
*Jacksonville Beach, FL & Los Angeles, CA – U.S.A.*
*www.DaltonCyr.com*

## "My Guardian Angel"

Music has helped me get through many difficult times. I always turn to my music when I need to express myself and reflect on the things going on in my life. My grandfather was my mentor and a major influence in teaching me about music. As a little girl, he gave me my first guitar and microphone and started me on guitar lessons. This time we shared together was very important to me. I looked forward to my lessons each day, and being able to share with him the notes and chords that I had learned. My grandfather was the one who helped me to develop my talents in music, and was one of my biggest supporters encouraging me to follow my dreams.

I was still young when my grandfather passed away from cancer. I was absolutely devastated. For a while, it was very hard for me to pick up the guitar again, knowing that he wouldn't be there to hear me play. After some time had passed, I finally picked up my guitar and sat down on the bed in my room. With the guitar cradled in my arms, I began to strum my fingers across the strings. As I continued to play, I could feel the presence of my grandfather sitting right next to me with that big smile on his face, watching with such pride. At that moment, I knew that he would always be there with me in spirit... cheering me on. I made a promise to him right then, and also to myself, that I would never stop using my music to express myself. I vowed that I would do everything I could to be a success in the music industry and make my grandfather proud.

Since then, I have continued writing music and now perform all around the world. I know that, whenever I perform my music, he is always there... watching over me as my guardian angel. I thank God every day for my amazing grandfather, the wonderful times we spent together, and most of all, for bringing music into my life.

*Darcy Donavan*
*Los Angeles, California – U.S.A.*
*www.DarcyDonavan.com*
*www.facebook.com/OfficialDarcyDonavan*

## MUSIC...you make my HEART SING!

## *"We're All In This Together"*

Whenever I hold an event, I bring in music to help set the mood for what I'm presenting that day. I find that playing music really helps motivate the audience to listen better and participate more in the event. Another place I always bring music is into hospital settings, particularly if I'm with a loved one or doing medical advocacy work. I set up whatever device I can, in the way of a boom box or an iPad, anything that can provide ongoing beautiful music, so that they will be motivated for healing. The research is so clear, and the results are absolutely stunning. If you sit there and watch the monitors, you can see very quickly how a patient's vital signs will show you the benefits of music. You can watch someone's heart rhythm slow down and begin to normalize; their blood pressure and breathing will also move towards healthier levels. You can truly engage a patient's mind, body and spirit through the power of music. I'm talking about people who are in Intensive Care and on a ventilator or some type of life support. It's just so powerful. The same thing with people in birthing rooms; women who are trying to deliver "big" human beings. Everybody needs to relax and be inspired.

My parents were born in 1921. When they were in their 70's and 80's, their health began to decline, resulting in various hospital trips. I was so happy that I had the freedom to bring music in to them. At the time, there were no iPads or other small devices, so I brought in a boom box to play their favorite music: romantic love songs. I remember so distinctly, seeing the reality come to life of what I had been studying as a psychologist. When people are hooked up to equipment, we can see their heart rate, blood pressure, respiration and we can see how much they are struggling or relaxing. If you sit with someone and hold their hand, play music or sing to them, it is amazing what happens to their physiology. I used to sit and watch the monitor equipment and the expressions on my parents' faces. At that point, music was pivotal for me... to see what it was that was so possible.

My dad, Warren Carlin, suffered from strokes and was only in his 70's when he passed in 1975. My parents loved music, so I grew up with a lot of the classics in our home. One of my dad's favorite's musicians was Louie Armstrong and one of his favorite songs was "What a Wonderful World". Louie Armstrong's voice is so rich and deep...the way he sings it really inspires people to feel the touch of life. When my dad was in the hospital, I would play songs and he and I would sing together. Even when he was dying, taking his last hours of breaths, I played music for him... helping him into a better space as he was making that transition.

There was a time, about 10 years before my mother passed away, where she had emergency surgery. Unfortunately, the surgery was botched, putting her on life support which was terrifying. When I showed up, I brought her favorite music into the Intensive Care Unit and played it almost continuously. There were also times when I would allow for quiet and peaceful moments (minus the machines in the room). I would hold my mother's hand, stroke her forehead gently, talk to her, and I would even sing to her. The song that I would sing with her the most was "Edelweiss", a song that presents a visual that is so inspiring...just envisioning the fields of beautiful flowers is breathtaking. I would hold her hand, sing and watch the reaction on her monitors. The staff would come in and sometimes sing along with me. When she later awoke, she told me what it was like to be on the receiving end of that and how it was absolutely "heaven". It was something that was so familiar to her and was done out of love. Really, there is nothing more powerful than true love.

One of the things I find so interesting, is how people will sometimes laugh at the theme of kindness; saying it's so fluffy and that psychology is soft science. It's intriguing to me, however, that some of our strongest and most admired icons are men who are songwriters and the tender themes that they write songs about the condition of the heart. It's all about love and connection, yet as a culture, we seem to be losing that valuable part of the message. When I was a kid in grade school, we would stand up every morning and sing the national anthem, or My Country Tis of Thee...America the Beautiful. We got in the habit of singing those together. I don't see that taking place in schools anymore. It's one of the things I wish we could return to doing...because it feels good, and not just because of the research. There has been so much going on around the globe these last several years. There are many peaceful things that tie us together, such as music. However, there is still too much violence in the way that many of us protest; all around the world we see riots happening, even in our country. There is a part of me that would like to fly helicopters all around and blast out really beautiful, peaceful, calming music to the crowds... infiltrate the crowds with the kind of music that everyone could participate in. There has to be a way to reach people's hearts who are so whipped up and frustrated. The way we seem to protest now doesn't result in anything productive happening. Remember the 60's when there were "sit-ins"; young people would protest by bringing their guitars and everyone would sit and sing. Now, there's this loud, stomping, throwing of rocks and insults...the protests have taken such a violent spin, when what's really needed is a call for peace and for justice. I wish music would be a part of it...something that delivers the message that *we are all in this together.*

*Dr. Deb Carlin*
*University City, Missouri – U.S.A.*
*The K Factor Radio Show www.DrDebCarlin.com*

## "Play Your Own Therapy"

Music has always been a part of my life. As a young child, I would check CD's out at the local library and listen intently, following the lyrics along in the booklets, and memorizing the words. Though I loved music, I was still an outsider to it. I had learned a few basic songs on guitar, but had never actually written anything of my own or performed. It wasn't until later that music would actually change me and help shape the person I would become.

When I was 14, I was diagnosed with a life altering disease, Juvenile Diabetes. Suddenly, I had the responsibility of regulating all my meals and giving myself shots. Eating was no longer something I looked forward to. Being a teenager is hard enough without the stress of this on top of it. There were times that I felt very depressed and wanted to die. My mother was concerned for me and tried to get me to go to counseling, but I refused. I didn't want to talk about it, because that would mean admitting I wasn't okay. I was good at hiding my depression from my friends and pretending I was dealing with the situation just fine.

When I refused counseling, my mom sent me to a camp for diabetic children. I begged her not to make me go. As a compromise, she let me take my best friend with me. She wasn't diabetic, but had medical problems of her own.

While at camp, my friend learned all the things I had to deal with. When camp was over, she wrote me a note. When I got home, I sat on my bed and read the note. It talked about how strong I was and how she didn't think she would be able to deal with it, if she was in my shoes. The words she'd written made me feel like crying. Even though I put on a front, I believed I wasn't that strong on the inside. I picked up my guitar and wrote my first song ever and called it "I'm Not that Strong". After writing it, I felt so much better and even more so after I started to play the song for others.

I began to use music as my therapy. Every time I had a problem in life, big or small, music was there for me. I wanted other young people to experience this too. So, when I was 16, I started interning with a group that provided grants for musicians who needed health care assistance. Within that organization, I founded a youth committee dedicated to helping young musicians learn all they needed to know about being a successful local musician. I also organized shows featuring musicians under 18. Though the organization has since dissolved, I am still working with youth and playing music myself.

Music helped me find my passion and finally make peace with myself. It may be cliché to say "Music saved my life", but that's exactly what it did. It also saved me a lot of therapy bills along the way.

*Elise Hofmann*
*Columbus, Ohio – U.S.A.*
*www.ReverbNation.com/EliseHofmann4*

---

**Music has an incredibly strong connection with math, which explains why many of the world's top scientists & mathematicians are also musicians.**

---

## "The Better You Get, The More You'll Enjoy It"

The summer my mother passed away, I went to Greenwood Music Camp in Northwestern, Massachusetts. At eleven years old, I was a wild kid, totally scattered and a pain in the ass for those charged with looking after me. I was also the incorrigible cellist of the resident Schmegeggie String Quartet, which consisted of the four youngest campers, all of whom seemingly also had the greatest aptitude for ADD. Our teacher was as much a sheepherder as a quartet coach. I played Crackabout (the genius outdoor sport invented at Greenwood which is 30% dodgeball, 30% soccer, 30% Ultimate Frisbee and 30% insanity) like I was possessed. I also had a love of cooking and often got in the way of the camp chef by hanging out in his kitchen at odd hours, happily peeling onions and flipping pancakes. I fell in love twice in two weeks: first with an amazing black lab named Zelda and then with an equally incredible blonde violinist. To impress her (the violinist), I determined to master the thing everyone at camp was doing and I started to take music more seriously. When I returned to Greenwood over the next few summers, I found myself enjoying the music more and more. I discovered that the more I practiced, the more love I had for music. This truth went hand in hand with a phrase my violinist father often said to me: "The better you get, the more you'll enjoy it."

The summer my mom died, my brother Colin was a counselor at Greenwood. No one could have dragged me to camp without him. I was always close to Colin, but after the sudden loss of our mother, we became much closer. He's four years older than me and I needed him near me for support, love and comfort. He saved me more than anyone by always being a constant and brotherly figure and, of course, by representing family and love.

Luckily my mother, consciously or not, had set up a

support system that made it possible for me to feel and act how I needed at that time. Friends and family who loved her, loved me. I was so fortunate to have this circle of support. In the span of a single Long Island summer day, I remember mourning with my family, playing hide-and-go-seek, then crying and then losing myself again in happiness with friends. I felt embarrassed that I was happy to be with friends.

Before camp, I'd felt embarrassed to cry in front of people outside of my family, but at Greenwood, nobody judged me or even paid much attention to the sudden bursts of whatever emotion I had to offer at that moment. I was also tasked with structured participation in a fun musical environment. Had I been left alone to weep, then that's all I would have done. Yet, had I not been allowed to explore pain, I would have bottled it up deep in my stomach. My brother and the other residents of the camp created an environment that let me feel comfortable in whatever emotion I was experiencing at the moment. At Greenwood that summer, I learned that none of those emotions were wrong. In fact, they are all called upon in life and in music.

The relationships that musicians have with older teachers and colleagues is quite unique. Even though classical music is taught with musical notation and interjected technical guidance from the composers themselves, the best way to learn the traditions and the spirit is through the aural teachings of mentors and those that have experienced the music firsthand. This is still another reason we are so lucky to play music: our very musicality is a result of the relationships we have. That summer at Greenwood, I started to see and hear music in a new light. This light would eventually illuminate a very clear path for my life.

At age eleven, I loved music because it represented family and love, and it was comforting. It still is, even as my own relationship to music has become more sophisticated and complex. My mother was a flutist and my father and brother are violinists. It took me awhile to realize the power of music and it continues to take me by surprise when I see life itself depicted in it. Performers are asked to use all of our collected emotions, from birth to death - often in a single, hour-long piece. Composers incorporate these feelings into their creations and an audience can internalize and empathize with these emotions throughout a performance.

Today, I can imagine what my life would be like if I was not a professional musician, but I can't imagine a life without music. I trace this love of music back to my family, my teachers, and to that summer - happy and sad - at Greenwood.

*Eric Jacobsen*
*Brooklyn, New York – U.S.A.*
*www.JacobsenEric.com*

## *"The Biggest Reward"*

I know music got me through a very difficult time in my life, a time when I may not have survived without it. I was born in Saigon, Vietnam and ended up in an orphanage as a baby. My parents came and adopted me at a time when I really needed someone to love me, hold me and bring stability to my life. My parents tell this story to me so I will remember how my life started and how I got to where I am now.

As a baby, it was really hard for me to fall asleep at night. I would scream, cry and bang my head against the wall. I suppose this was a way for me to go to sleep in the orphanage without someone there to hold me and sing lullabies. It was just a dark place with lots of babies crying out for a mommy to come and comfort them. My whole world changed when my parents brought me home to America. They held me tight and showered me with the love that every child deserves. They also discovered that music was a great way to calm me, and help me go to sleep without being afraid. Every night, my dad would hold me on his shoulder and sing to me, until I fell asleep. This could take a long time in the beginning, but eventually, I would fall asleep after an hour or so.

It wasn't long before my parents had me play with different kinds of musical instruments, anything that I could make noise with. I must have liked this, as I began playing the violin when I was four years old, without objection. I would have to play at recitals, and I think that experience really gave me the courage to perform in front of audiences. I remember hearing them applaud after I played, which really made me feel good. I liked that! I could feel my confidence building, my public speaking getting better and my love for music exploding into something that would drive me to be the best.

Well, now I am 15 years old and perform as first violinist in several orchestras. I also have found a love for singing and have begun putting that to good use. Last year, I competed for Miss Delaware's Outstanding Teen and won. I also won first place in talent (singing) for both the local and state competitions. As Miss Delaware's Outstanding Teen, my platform is Musical Therapy for Alzheimer's patients, where I visit nursing homes and perform for them by singing and playing my violin. I learn old songs from the 40's and 50's that they can relate to, and many times get responses such as foot or hand tapping, and sometimes they even sing along with me. The biggest reward for me however, is just seeing them smile whenever I sing and play.

Although, I have come a long way with music in my life, I know there is much left to my journey. My motto in life is: *"God's gift to me is my musical talent. Using my talent to benefit others is my gift to God"*.

*Grace Otley*
*Wilmington, Delaware – U.S.A.*
*www.Reverbnation.com/GraceOtley*

## *"To All Purple Tree Trunks"*

While working on the West Coast, I made a friend who was in high school and having complex personal problems. It was a very stressful situation and her family didn't know how to be supportive in the ways she needed. As a result, she became suicidal. She later told me that the one thing that kept her alive was the song "To All Purple Tree Trunks." It was a song I wrote and performed back then that basically gives us all permission to just be ourselves. My friend is now grown and successfully living in New York with a hope-filled future. Here's an excerpt from the song:

"Here's to all purple tree trunks
Long may they grow
Here's to wild, crazy colors
Where the lines never go
It might be that you're seeing
What no one's ever seen
Normal is just a setting on your washing machine."

*Jack Pearson*
*Minneapolis, Minnesota – U.S.A.*
*www.JackPearson.org*

## *"Singing for Baby"*

Although I'm only 12 years old, music is already a big part of who I am. My father had an Alan Jackson CD he listened to a lot when I was five and I would always sing along. It wasn't long before I knew all the words to every song. I must have been the only five year old who was singing, "It's Five O'clock Somewhere" in my Kindergarten class!

I come from a family of music lovers and I'm always humming or singing a song. My mother loves to sing and play guitar and her father (my grandfather), Tommy Ferguson, was a professional musician. My Great Aunt, Eileen Maurizio, was a professional singer and her husband (my Uncle), Hank Maurizio, was a professional drummer.

Over the past year, I took my love of singing from out of the shower to performing in public for the very first time. It all started with my school's Talent Show. During that time, I was dealing with the loss of our horse, Baby. I was very close to her and though I was initially scared to sing in public, I decided to sing in her memory. Singing for my horse, Baby, gave me the strength to get up on that stage and give it all I had. I still talk to her every time before I perform...I know she is listening. As a result, I discovered that I LOVE performing. I also love that I get to meet so many amazing people. Without music, I would never have that opportunity.

My love for singing and performing is a wonderful outlet and a great comfort for me. Whether it's school pressures or dealing with bullies, music is always there for me. When I'm having a bad day or feeling stressed, I can pick up my guitar I recently learned to play, start strumming some chords and sing away. It is truly incredible how powerful music can be.

I am so thankful to God for the love and support I have from my family, who I love more than anything on this earth; for my friends who truly care for me, for my dreams and, of course, the gift of music.

*Julia Zane*
*Glenolden, Pennsylvania – U.S.A.*

## *"The Power to Heal"*

For six years I performed for and served on the Advisory Board of Pickleberry Pie, a non-profit organization that presents musical programs to children in hospital settings throughout the U.S. IN 2014 I was asked to perform at the University of Virginia's Children's Hospital - a beautiful facility, with a dedicated staff. The day I arrived, many children were too ill to leave their beds, so I visited their rooms instead. I was told that one small girl had not smiled or shown any emotion in several weeks. Yet, as soon as I started to play my guitar and sing, she laughed and let out a small cry of joy. Her mother, several staff members and I all simultaneously burst into tears. Later that day, a group of patients and their families gathered for a short performance. An eight year old boy who had been lethargic for several days, lifted his arms from his wheelchair and squealed in delight. Even though his IVs were still attached, He tried his best to clap along to the music. For just a few minutes, these children were free of pain...free of pain...thanks to the power of music.

Another time, while performing for military families in Europe with the U.S. Department of Defense, I was asked to sing for the first three soldiers who had been wounded on the front lines in Iraq. Having just arrived from a long overseas flight, I was jet-lagged and concerned that my children's songs wouldn't be appropriate. I visited them all that night, playing several of my own songs, plus a group request for Pete Seeger's song, "If I Had a Hammer!" I even sung one soldier to sleep with one of my lullabies!

Fast forward to three years later...I was on tour in California when a guy came up to me with his four-year old daughter. He asked if I knew who he was, and I said, "Sorry, I don't recall." He said, "Do you remember singing me to sleep in the hospital at Ramstein?" I immediately burst into tears while thanking him for his service, hugged his daughter, gave them a CD, and then he thanked ME for helping him heal!

Even in my own family, music has had a big impact. In 1999, my niece was accidentally buried in a sand tunnel some children had dug into the banks of Lake Alcova in Wyoming. When she was finally located, she was unconscious, oxygen-deprived and flown by a Flight for Life helicopter to the nearest hospital in Casper, Wyoming. We were not sure she was going survive, or just how or if her brain would heal if she did. I was on tour in Europe and unable to return while she was in ICU, but I had my sister (her mother) take my cd's to her nurses and play them for her. Although she had been unresponsive for a week, one nurse later told me that she kicked her legs and squeezed her hands when she heard my songs. Unbelievably, even in her coma-like state, my music helped prompt some of her first movements. Today, my amazing niece is happily married and going strong as a new mother, and working as a wind–energy consultant. Yes, indeed, music does have the power to heal.

*Katherine Dines*
*Denver, Colorado – U.S.A.*
*Hunk-Ta-Bunk-Ta Music*
*www.HunkTaBunkTa.com*

> # Songs help us remember the people and places that mean the most to us.

## *"Music is My Lifeline & I Can't Stop Creating"*

I am a 42-year old award-winning, quirky, folk, pop singer-songwriter, recording artist, performer and playwright from San Francisco. I also have been battling a rare auto-immune disease since 2008: Dermatomyositis (DM). I turned to music and art as a healing path and ended up inspiring others. My story is one of persevering through this darkness called DM by way of the creative process...starting as a singer-songwriter and later becoming a Muse. Music is my Lifeline and I literally can't stop creating!

My Artist name is Aoede (pronounced A-E-D), which means "song" in Greek. Aoede was the first Muse of Song in Greek Mythology. When I chose the name in 2005, I wanted an affiliation with this particular muse as a reminder to be inspired and to continually inspire. This theme has resonated with me, even more, over the last few years and has become a central theme in my life. Due to life throwing me some unexpected curveballs, I have become a muse to many in ways I never expected: offering support, compassion, inspiration, connection and encouragement to those who need it most. By sharing my music & art and telling my own story, I have discovered others are inspired to tell theirs, and in many cases, pursue some passion or joy that's inside their hearts.

Dermatomyositis is a progressive muscle weakness disease affecting stamina, energy, skin and muscles. If untreated, DM attacks and weakens my immune system and muscles, as well as, my mind and spirit. I've been dealing with the challenges of managing this condition, trying to find just the right combination of treatments, drugs and therapies, along with a slower pace and a lot of naps, since April 2008. The worst of it was a flare-up in 2010, when I was hospitalized for 24 days. I never could have guessed just how much music would play a role in my healing.

Part of my hospitalization involved 12 days of rehabilitation, which included occupational therapy. I recall one session where I mentioned I was a singer-songwriter and that I really wanted to play and sing again. The staff person brought in his kid's guitar, and I remember how hard it was even for me to hold that small guitar. I tried singing my song "What You Got," which was my anthem throughout this whole storm of a hospital experience. "When life is hurling lemons at you; when you're so tired you can't get out of bed; whatever life throws at you, you've got to pick yourself up and do what you can with what you got!" I wrote this song in 2010 to instill hope and encouragement in others and, I suppose, myself as well. During this rehab stint, I could barely sing and play, but playing that guitar and singing renewed something in me. It was like, "I'm going to be ok. I will get through this. And this is what I've got right now to give..."

I remember laying in a hospital chair during my first IVIG (immunoglobulin) experience. Those God-awful florescent lights were glaring over me and I was thinking "Please God, let me get through this." Why I was so freaked out, I cannot say. I did the only things I could think to do, I slowed my breathing and concentrated on each breath. I held my husband, Dave's, hand. I let myself be in that yucky, medicated space because I knew I had no choice. And then, when my heart was racing so fast it felt like it was coming out of my chest, I began to sing. The words just came out. In retrospect, I guess it was the one thing I knew deep inside that would release me from that place of fear, from anxiety, from hospital space. I sang the first verse of a new song that I had recently written "If You Already Knew":

*What if you were born,*
*Knowing how your life would unfold*
*Where you'd skin your knees*
*When you'd see your first rainbow*
*What if you couldn't choose*
*What you'd say or do*
*There'd be no surprises or waiting for signs*
*If you already knew*

I couldn't have dreamed up more appropriate words to speak to my heart. All I knew was I had to sing and I knew then, somehow, I would get through this.

From the time I returned home from the hospital, I was trying to figure out how to get my music out into the world. This was my focus while physical and occupational therapists were coming to the house, family and friends shuttled me back and forth to the hospital for infusions, and while I was learning a new norm that involved wheelchairs, walkers, ramps, commode seats and shower benches. I found myself retaining a PR firm, developing a new website, doing a photo shoot, taking up ukulele, shooting a music video, starting my first blog Dermatowhat?, engaging on social networks, recording music and giving radio interviews. All of this, except for parts of the music video shoot, I did from home - mostly from bed.

Yet, when my publicity folks were fishing around for an angle to help promote my music, I struggled for ideas. I mentioned in passing, I wasn't really doing live shows due to some health issues; that I had been in the hospital and at home recovering. "No performances? No tours?

Where's the story?" It took my PR directly probing me to make me realize just what my story was. Here's how he framed it: "So, you said you were in the hospital for 24 days right? Yeah. Wow. People who get heart bypasses are out in just a few days now. 24 days huh? And you are releasing an album? All while going back and forth for doctor appointments and infusions and physical therapy"?

I got it. As he asked the questions, I blurted out of nowhere with certainty and passion "Music is my lifeline!" as the tears began to well up inside and finally spill out because at last, I understood what I, Aoede, the muse of song, was here to do...I truly got it. I suddenly knew my story. My story is one of persevering through this darkness called DM using the creative process. Music is my Lifeline, and I cannot stop creating.

Here's what's wild: when my story began to become public, it's as if I started attracting the very people who needed the light - some with DM, but also others! I found that, when I allowed myself to be vulnerable, it opened doors for others to tell their stories, and for me to be a muse in ways I had never expected.

I wrote the song Perfect Day in June 2011 after communicating with a bed-ridden fan that also suffers from a debilitating muscle disease. He is constantly in need of breathing support, yet finds empowerment and motivation through activities from his bed. When I first read his story, it brought me to tears. Then my muse started to flow and out came Perfect Day, imagining the world through his lens. What I realized is, it wasn't just his journey I was lamenting; it was my own. It was the first time I let myself feel in song what I had gone through; to acknowledge my own limitations. I have since partnered with CureJM, the kid version of the same disease I have, to help raise awareness and to give back. I created a music video for "Perfect Day" that features CureJM warriors as superheroes, and have led a session on using art and music as a healing path at CureJM's conference.

"Award winning singer-songwriter Aoede is no stranger to overcoming obstacles and realizing her dreams" wrote Christopher Ewing, Metro Media Group.

If I had a crystal ball in 2011, I would have seen that coming. I would have also known that in just a few years I'd have released 5 albums, been considered for Grammy Awards, become a playwright, written and recorded three fantasy musicals (staged one) and received over 40 songwriting awards for my music and art. I know now, that I will always be using music & art to heal myself and inspire others to do whatever is in their souls. I've now lived with DM for eight years. Most days, I like to immerse myself in my place of joy: my musical world. I like to forget I live with a rare disease. The reality is, I live with DM and it is part of me and without it, maybe I wouldn't have started dreaming so big in the first place. I try to show, by example, that having a chronic illness doesn't mean you can't have dreams. Maybe they change from what they once were, but without a dream to follow, who are we really?

*Lisa Sniderman (Aoede)*
*San Francisco, California – U.S.A.*
*www.aoedemuse.com*

---

**I FEEEEEEL GOOOOD - And it's all thanks to MUSIC!!**

## "The Power of Music"

Towards the end of 2014, I was invited by Nordoff Robbins (a music therapy based charity) to come along and witness, first hand, the amazing work that they do with all kinds of people suffering from various disabilities. On arrival at their North West London HQ, I was taken into a small observation room, to the side of one of the many classrooms there. On that morning, class was being held for 4 young children aged between 4 and 5 years old. Their disabilities ranged from neurological to severe physical handicaps. It was immediately apparent that each of them had tremendous difficulty communicating with the world around them. As the session began, I was touched by how engaged the children became; not just with their caregivers, but with each other. They especially enjoyed interacting with the music therapists performing for them. These musicians weren't just playing songs for them, they were helping the children actually join in on the music making that they so obviously loved to hear. If I ever needed evidence that music is so powerful and so spiritual, then here it was in action. Truly amazing.

*Mark King*
*www.Level42.com*
*@King42Mark*

## "Music Brought My Mother Back to Me"

I have been working and living with music all my life. As far back as I can remember, music has been inseparable from my thinking. Even as a child, I recall commenting to an uncle that I had a peculiar sense that there was always a tune playing unconsciously in my head, day and night. Oftentimes, it was the last song I had heard or sung, but there always was music playing in the background of my life. To this day, this is still true. Music became even more integral to my life when I became a professional musician.

The most emotional experience I have ever had with music occurred soon after my mother came down with the dreaded Alzheimer's disease. Throughout her life, my mother was just as inspired and moved by music as I am. My father was also very inspired by music, and like me, almost always seemed to have a tune stuck in his head. My mother, however, is the one who was the motivating force in enrolling me at the Santiago Conservatory of Music in my native Cuba. I started violin classes at the early age of 8. Although I never really followed up with my violin, this experience gave me the formal music training that later helped me to learn how to play the guitar and lead my salsa band.

My mother and father initially moved here to Pittsburgh from Erie, PA to spend their retirement years close to my own family. After a rich & brilliant career as a high school teacher and college professor, my mother came down with Alzheimer's at the age of 65. This was right at the time she should have begun enjoying her golden retirement years with my father. Prior to this, she had been a vibrant, alert and highly intelligent scholar. Her research paper on the role of Latin American Spanish language children's nursery rhymes and children's playground songs, completed in the 1960's, can still be found on the internet today. As her disease progressed, it wasn't long before she could not be left alone, not even for a moment. Without someone to keep a close eye on her, she would wander off into the street and very quickly get lost. By the late 1980's, she was largely very passive and unresponsive. She would simply follow along quietly wherever she was led, without much expression or emotion.

One evening, I took charge of my mother so my father could have the night off and go to his beloved Chess Club meeting. I was driving her from the club in Squirrel Hill, back to my own house in Bloomfield. We were stopped at a traffic light on Bigelow Boulevard, not far from the Bloomfield Bridge. She sat quietly next to me in the front passenger seat, not responding to my words to her and with no expression on her face. I absentmindedly began to hum an old song by a Puerto Rican author, which had been popular during her youth. Suddenly, as if by magic, my mother came back to life next to me! She turned to face me and smiled. She began to sing the words to the song and move her body to the rhythm. I laughed out loud and sang along with her. She could barely remember my name, but here she was, singing every lyric & melody to this rhythmic Latin song. Simply unbelievable!

My mom lived with that horrible mind-robbing disease for many years after that time, until she died in 2013. But to me, the most memorable moment between her and I is still that brief instant on Bigelow Boulevard; that one special moment when a song from her youth brought my mother back to me from the depths of Alzheimer's...a moment when she and I sang together once again, just like when I was a child.

*Miguel Sague*
*Pittsburgh, Pennsylvania – U.S.A.*
*www.CaneyCircle.OwlWeb.org*

## *"A Quiet, Driving Force Inside of Me"*

I first became interested in music at around the age of 10. My brother and I would often make cardboard guitars, and attach rubber bands to try and play old Jamaican gospel tunes. My mother would sing around the house and my dad would often hum the bass parts while cooking or doing chores.

Growing up, I attended a Jamaican Pentecostal church that featured a full band set up, including a Hammond organ, guitar, bass and drums. Brother Jones ran the choir and the band. His son, Steven Jones, was a good friend of mine and played bass.

My first musical love was the guitar, followed closely by the drums. However, the deciding factor in me playing the bass guitar happened one Sunday during a church convention when I was just 12 years old. Brother Jones came down to my dad's house to ask if I could come and play bass. For some reason, Steven wasn't available that day and they needed a replacement. He had seen me playing the bass after the church service and was surprised how I was able to keep up, playing only by ear. This ability was due to hearing my dad accompany my mum by humming the bass all while I was growing up. I was really excited that he asked me, but remember feeling scared at the same time. That day, I played bass in the band, while a couple hundred people sang their hearts out. I enjoyed this experience deep, deep down into my soul and I knew, from then on, all I wanted to do was play the bass guitar. It was a feeling so strong, that it became a quiet driving force inside of me, one that is still there to this day...some 40 years later.

There have been many difficult times throughout my life where music has helped me; from normal everyday stresses where music offered a comforting backdrop, to times of severe sadness. My sister, whom I loved dearly, died very suddenly 6 years ago from stomach cancer; from the time she began to feel ill to the time she passed away was just 6 weeks. She, like all my siblings, loved music. I would sometimes make compilations of various songs for her that I knew she loved. As her illness progressed, I would sit with her, and we would both cry, knowing she was going to die. I would play music for her that I knew she loved and together we would smile. On the night of her funeral, her family and friends all gathered together; I was the DJ and played all the music we knew she treasured. That night was a powerful experience that helped many of us begin to heal. I still listen to this music now and always will; sometimes with sadness, but mostly with happiness as I imagine her smile.

Another situation that really affected me occurred when I was in Durban, South Africa visiting a small HIV clinic. While sitting in an office chair, a small choir came in and sang with such incredible joy. Despite the beautiful music their voices made, I could still see the sadness in their eyes as they tried to cope with what had become a normal life for them. After experiencing this, I couldn't help but cry.

Creating music, in addition to playing and listening to it, has always helped me find a way to keep level headed. As a touring musician, needing to leave your family on a regular basis quickly becomes the norm. For me, music has always seemed to come first. At times, it has come before family, friends, pets, parties, homework, girls, sports, everything. As a result, my life is constantly changing and I never know where the next turn will be. I am, however, very grateful to make a living doing what I absolutely love. My passion for music has taken me to places all around the world and helped me see and experience things that otherwise, would never be possible.

*Pete Shand*
*Bassist, The New Mastersounds, 1999 - Present*
*www.NewMastersounds.com*

---

# The quickest way to someone's heart, is very often through a song.

---

### *"Therapy for the Performer Too"*

I've been a performer now for the past 20 years or more. About 4 years ago, my musical partner, Dan Kleiman, died suddenly of a stroke. Dan was an extraordinary pianist, composer and the musical director of our world jazz ensemble SIORA. Perhaps, even more importantly, he was my best friend. After he died, we had a very busy concert schedule still planned, so I had to quickly find a substitute pianist. Even more challenging, was that I now had to learn to lead the band, which was quite daunting for me. The process of learning to stand on my own 2 musical feet and to keep going, was truly a godsend for me during my grieving process. I gradually felt my own strength growing and not a moment too soon. Almost immediately after Dan's passing, I began to go through the long and painful process of watching my husband die of a rare case of early onset dementia. Crazy stuff life presents to us sometimes. But through it all, I've learned to count my blessings and to find opportunities in the face of tragedy.

For years, I've had the good fortune to have people come up to me saying how they've been touched by my music. Now, through my own personal experience, I have to say that singing and performing music is therapy in and of itself - just the act of making music. Through this whole process, I also wrote a few very poignant songs, which I know were - and still are - cathartic for me. I feel truly blessed to have music be a part of my life.

*Phyllis Chapell*
*Bala Cynwyd, Pennsylvania – U.S.A.*
*www.SioraJazz.com*

## *"Marching Beyond Halftime"*

Music has been a critical part of my life, ever since I can remember. I was born and raised in Orlando, Florida and had a wonderful music education in all my public schools. But even before that, I had a very unique music education taught by a very special teacher. My Grandma Rose Flatow, from New York City, used to come to town and spend long periods of time with us. She taught me the basics when I was very little. In fact, I learned to read and write music well before I could read or write English. She taught me how to draw a musical staff and a treble clef. She even taught me how to read the notes "Every Good Boy Does Fine" and "FACE". I would listen to Grandma Rose talk to me for hours about opera, Broadway musicals and classical music. I was in awe, as we would listen to records and she would tell me stories about all of the happenings at Lincoln Center, just up the street from her. She instilled in me a deep reverence for music and the arts that I have carried always.

As I mentioned, I was extremely fortunate to have a solid music education from kindergarten through college. I was in chorus and musical theater in elementary school. I was also in band during middle school, high school and throughout my college years at the University of Florida. I loved it all: the rehearsals, the performances, practicing by myself for hours in pursuit of perfection and, of course, the camaraderie. My closest friends, to this day, are those that I performed with in band.

After graduating college, I moved to Los Angeles, California to pursue work in the entertainment industry, which ultimately, lead to my career as a producer. I create behind the scenes content for DVDs, TV and other media. I've been fortunate to work (and have worked) on some of the most successful films and shows on television including *Grey's Anatomy*, *Desperate Housewives*, *Scandal* and *How To Get Away With Murder*. All along, my musical background and training have proved critical to my success.

However, I really didn't understand the true impact of music on my life until January 2012, when I was diagnosed with breast cancer. The experience was terrifying on every level. At the beginning of my journey, I was grasping for anything that could ease the trauma. I learned quickly that I had to go back to the basics in order to get through this. THAT'S when it all started coming together. I realized that the tools and the connections that I learned through the arts, particularly from my years in band, were what would carry me through.

One of the first things I noticed was that many of my band friends came out of the woodwork to be there for me; some I had not spoken to in almost 30 years. Their encouragement and support was incredibly soothing.

Then, there were some of the practical skills. The breathing exercises that I would tire of in school, now proved invaluable as they helped get me through some of the most uncomfortable procedures. My leadership skills helped me navigate and lead the team of doctors and the administrative parts of this adventure. This was huge!

But, most importantly, was the music itself. One of the most powerful experiences for me was listening to music during my ordeal. I had 9 surgeries, countless procedures, months of daily IV infusions and many unexpected trips to the hospital. No matter how difficult the circumstances were or how terrible I felt, the one thing I was always able to do, was to listen to music. I can't even begin to verbalize what a comfort it was. I truly believe that all of these things are what carried me through.

And now, three years later, I am well on the road to recovery. Inspired by the impact that music has had in my own life, I am now creating a documentary on the power of music education; it's called *Marching Beyond Halftime*. I want to show audiences how a solid music education has far reaching and long lasting effects on a person's life, in wherever life leads them. I know it has for me!

*Sara Flatow*
*Los Angeles, California – U.S.A.*
*Producer/Director - Marching Beyond Halftime*
*www.MarchingBeyondHalftime.com*

## "Heaven's Gate"

Music, to me, is extremely therapeutic and a wonderful outlet to help explain our feelings and emotions It allows us to create something tangible that others can listen to and, very often, relate with.    Through my own hard times and struggles, music has gotten me through by allowing me to pour my feelings into something positive.  Other people listen and sometimes say "Oh Wow, I'm going through the same thing."   I feel that we all connect through music...we all feel the same types of things, and I think that's very important.

I was just about to turn 10 years old, when my Mom passed away.   When I was 12, I wrote the song "Heaven's Gate" to help me remember and to show my appreciation for her...she was a great person.    It was a very difficult experience to go through, but I have great memories of my Mom and family...those are the things that I hold on to. Struggles like that definitely help make you stronger and, unfortunately, it's something everyone has to go through at some point.  In the end, you just have to tough it out...it helps makes you a stronger person.

Many times, while I was performing, someone in the audience would start to cry and come up to me afterwards.  Often, it was the song I wrote for my Mom, and you could see how much they were really moved by it; either because I lost my Mom or because they themselves lost someone close.  It's very humbling to me to see how songs I've written can really touch someone.  I can't tell you how much that means to me.   When you're writing a song, you don't think that it's going to relate to someone else.  You kinda just do it, because it's what you're feeling at the time...only later do you realize that so many people go through those same experiences.  When that happens, you start to relate to them on a personal level.  Like I said, we all connect though music and I don't think there's anything else in this world that makes us more human.

*"Heaven's Gate"*

*About 9 years old, just a little girl*
*Playing exploring in this great big world*
*Just having fun*
*Got in a little fight with my mom,*
*Didn't know how long she was fighting*
*Trying to hold on strong*

*Mama woke me up with a kiss*
*She said I gotta go but remember this*
*She said I'll always love you so*
*Found out the news the next day*
*Daddy said she had to go away*
*My heart broke and my life changed*

*But I had to move on*
*And I had to be strong*
*Everything changed*
*When my momma passed away*
*But it's okay*
*Momma's in a better place*
*And I know I'll be with her one day*
*Yeaaaah Heaven's Gate...*

*Sara Spicer*
*Folsom, Pennsylvania – U.S.A.*
*www.SaraSpicer.com*

## "How I Found the Real Me"

Music has become very important to me, and at one point, actually helped sustain my life. I had gone through a very bad time in 1996. I had a very nice life of riding my horses and developing a wonderful horse business. I really enjoyed the whole process of riding, training, breeding and teaching. Most of all, I loved learning what made a horse tick. At the same time, I had been having some neck issues for years that I finally needed to address. I saw several doctors with most telling me to do exercises and a few telling me surgery might be the answer.

To make a long story short, I eventually had the operation on my neck. That day, my life changed and I did an about face, a complete 180. When I awoke from the surgery, I had no idea how much my life was going to be in jeopardy over the next two weeks or what this doctor was going to put me through. After having cervical spinal surgery, I was about to go on a journey that no one should have to endure. I had complications from the moment I woke up that ranged from initially not being able to feel my thumb, and then soon after, having trouble feeling my leg and arm. I kept having progressively worse pain in my left arm and neck area, and all during this time the doctor kept telling me that I was fine and not to worry. I was discharged from the hospital, but was quickly back in the Emergency Room where, once again, no tests were run and I was simply put under observation. Then, very quickly, I was dismissed to go home again and my health began to decline even faster.

Finally, I was taken to Paoli Memorial Hospital, where the emergency doctors there were astonished at my condition and asked who did this to me. From that point, they began the process of helping to save my life. Otherwise, I probably would have died. I had a very bad staph infection, a huge spinal abscess and osteomyelitis, which is a bone infection. I needed several additional surgeries, then spent weeks in the hospital and then rehab for a year with a lot of complications.

It wasn't until a year later that I started to go out to a country club and sing with the piano player, Jerry, just for fun. I was still doing rehab and dealing with lingering health problems, but I began to look forward to singing whenever I could. Soon, everywhere I went, people would ask me to sing. One day I was up in Maine with my family and I was singing "Crazy" by Patsy Cline in a local piano bar. A very nice man approached me and said "You need to meet my sister in Nashville, Tennessee. She is always looking for great singers to do demos". I was like, "Oh no not me, I just enjoy singing". I chuckled, took his sister's card and ended up giving her a call 6 months later. Within another 6 months, I found myself flying down to Nashville where a whole new life began to open up for me. I could really start to feel what music was doing for me. Healing me, taking me by the hand and showing me there is this inner strength that felt like it was coming from music itself. Music pulls you in and then let's you go with a beautiful thread attached to your soul. I became music and music became me.

After this whole ordeal, people often ask me about my transformation. My reply is simple: "While trying to recreate me, the person who I became was someone who I really never met before, and it was all because of music". I feel like I met the real "me" for the first time when I wrote my first song.

Singing, playing and writing music helps us to express what is going on deep inside, and that is the engine that begins the healing process that so many of us need.

*Suzanne Dee Gorman*
*Nashville, Tennessee – U.S.A.*
*www.FaceBook.com/SuzanneDee25*
*www.ReverbNation.com/SuzanneDeeGorman*

## "Music Lifts Us, When Nothing Else Can"

I have been teaching music and movement classes in my daughter's school on Fridays for over four years now. It has, by far, become my most favorite day of the week. It's not that it's easy; in fact, quite the contrary – it is quite challenging and requires a lot of energy.

There are about 100 - 150 kids in each group. They are all so excited and wound up that, sometimes, controlling the chaos is, well...let's just say, it can get quite loud. My class consists of 45 minutes of call and response songs, rhythm games, circle dances, creative movement and original music. My goals are always the same - to allow these kids to have some freedom of movement, to learn new songs, reinforce language skills and to find the joy in singing and dancing. The kids all come around, eventually, and do what I ask them to do. It makes me feel as if I have accomplished something important at the close of each class. Part of the joy that I get out of it, is the satisfaction of being able to handle such an enthusiastic crowd of 5 to 7 year olds and to have them walk away singing new songs and wearing smiles on their faces.

In this school, there are 2 classrooms of special needs children. My schedule allows me to spend a little extra time with them in their rooms after the large groups. I feel very fortunate to have this time with them. They seem to really like being able to touch the guitar and have their questions answered in a more intimate setting.

After my first "one-on-one" class with them a few years ago, I left feeling a bit confused. I knew that they enjoyed my class, but wondered if I was really going to be able to make a difference or was it all just going to be entertainment? A few weeks after that class, I was in the middle of teaching my second large group of the day, my Pre-K and K classes. I then saw one of my special needs students walk by the door in the hallway. Well, he didn't really walk by, he actually stopped still in the doorway, turned to the group and began actively listening to the music. His Physical Therapist (PT) was there with him, so I assumed they were on their way to a session. This little boy (we'll call him Johnny) stayed in the doorway for quite some time so I waved to him. He smiled and waved back. A few seconds later, I saw his PT speak to him and then Johnny came in and joined the group. He sat right down in the middle of another class (with children that he did not know) and began to participate. All of the teachers and children made him feel welcome and he stayed for the rest of the class. Later that day, his PT came up to me and said, "That was quite amazing with what happened with Johnny." "Oh?" I said. "I'm sorry if I took him away from your session. Thank you for letting him participate." "Well, I didn't have a choice" he told me. "Johnny stood there in the doorway and would not follow me and then informed me that he was going to your class instead," he said with a smile. "Really?" I asked. "Yes. And did you see what happened after your performance?" "No, I didn't see." I answered. "Normally, after our sessions, Johnny doesn't walk up the stairs. He can walk down, no problem, but he doesn't ever go up. He complains and drags his feet. Most times I have to help him, or even carry him, back up to his classroom." "Oh, I didn't know that." I said. I wasn't really sure where this story was going. "So, after your performance, he turned to me and said 'Good show!' and walked straight up to his classroom!" I looked at him. He had a glowing look on his face as he looked directly at me. I then realized that I had tears in my eyes. I guess the most profound thing that I took away from that experience was the fact that music and movement heal us without necessarily labeling them as "therapy."

My experience that day contributed to my decision to go back to school to learn more about the benefits of music and movement therapies. As it turns out, it's really quite simple. Every day, we are moved by music that we listen to on the subway, on our IPods, in the home or car... in order to gear up for our day. We experience a release when we dance and allow our bodies to "just move to the beat" without caring if we are doing the right steps. We stretch in yoga classes and chant OM to allow our minds and bodies to connect and be as one. Why? Because, when we have access to music and movement, we are happier. We feel better. We laugh more. We have more of a connection to others and to ourselves. Our hearts become open, allowing the happiness and joy to help us heal. This is why I love music. This is why I love dance. It's the reason I teach music and movement and also why I write and perform for children and families. It's a big part of what makes us all human.

*Suzi Shelton*
*Brooklyn, New York – U.S.A.*
*www.SuziShelton.com*

## *"Forever Gone But Never Forgotten"*

Music is my life and plays a part in all of my most special moments; my happiness, my sadness, my defeat, my most passionate love – For all of these times, music has always been there. That's why I am an artist. All of the most substantial moments of my life, one way or another, have been impacted by music and I hope my music can help do that for others.

It all started when I was 9 years old. Writing was the only way I was able to express myself when my young brother passed away. I sat down one day, and without even realizing it, wrote a song. To this day, I still perform that song and listen to it in my darkest of times, to remind myself to keep going and tell others that losing someone is okay. That there is a brighter light at the end of the tunnel. That song is called "Forever Gone".

Music is not only heard in your times of despair. Some of my greatest pieces were written from being in love or just being happy. I have written music to be positive. To Stop Bullying. To be strong. To stay alive. To smile. I have written music for the man I love. For the mother I adore. For even that fun night at the teen club...LOL! Music is made for you. To tell your story. To share a moment and connect with people around the world who have felt the way you have and who dream the way you do. To reveal yourself in ways you couldn't have ever thought of. Music makes YOU.

"Believe In Yourself, Follow Your Dreams, Become the VeRoleModel Everyone looks up to!"

*Veronica Kole – Teen Pop Artist*
*Freehold, New Jersey – U.S.A.*
*www.VeronicaKoleOfficial.com*
*@Veronica_Kole*

## *"No Matter What, Write a Song About It"*

My earliest memory of music was my father and uncle playing their acoustic guitars together whilst singing and harmonizing. The beautiful sounds they made together blew my mind. I began studying music, followed by voice, very shortly after that enlightening encounter. It wasn't until I was working as a professional vocalist that music became my obsession and one that ultimately saved my life.

My former record producer and mentor, the late Kim Fowley (The Murmaids, The Runaways, Alice Cooper) always told me that no matter what was happening in my life, I should "write a song about it". He taught me music in a way I had never learned before and he helped me listen to music in a way I had never heard before. I treasure the time that I had working with both Kim and David Carr (The Fortunes, The Ventures). The recording sessions and music we made together were some of the most thrilling moments of my career and I will never forget them. At one point in my life, I was hospitalized and almost died due to kidney failure. While I was there, I laid in my room thinking "I can't die. What about all the music I've yet to create?" I realized then, that even in the very darkest hour, the music must always play. I then wrote a song in that same hospital bed that inspired me to live another day, just to have the opportunity to record it when I was released.

Now, on my darkest days of whatever fear, doubt and pain life is throwing me, I write a song about it. Music is my greatest passion and the recording studio is my church. To be able to write and create music every day is a blessing.. When I can't exactly say what "it" is that I want to say, I simply say it with music. I now have an "eighth note" tattoo on the top of my left wrist in the shape of a cloud being wrapped by a rainbow to eternally remind me.

Without music, I just wouldn't be the same. It has made me a better person and it continues to inspire me to evolve, each and every day.

*Victoria De Mare*
*Los Angeles, California – U.S.A.*
*Artist, Vocalist, Composer, Arranger*
*Music Producer & Publisher*
*www.ScreamQueenDeMare.com*


## *"Will I Be Able to Play the Guitar Ever Again?"*

My son Michael's passion for music probably saved his life. As a young boy, we were able to see his enthusiasm for music in almost everything he did. When he was thirteen, he picked up his first guitar and started playing almost immediately. In October 2011, Michael auditioned for "Americas Got Talent". The producer loved him so much as a guitarist, that she wanted him to incorporate vocals into his act. Michael had always played music eight hours a day, but now, he spent every available minute practicing. He had been given a challenge to learn to sing over the next thirty days. His love for music lead him to do just that.

As the family celebrated Christmas that year, we were all excited to see if Michael was selected for the show. Unlike most sixteen year olds, Michael gave up any kind of social life to keep practicing. However, during Christmas dinner, Michael asked if he could go out for an hour; his friend had just received a car as a Christmas present. Since he worked so hard following his dream, we decided to let him go.

As my wife and I sat in front of the fire enjoying our tree, the phone rang. When my wife answered it, I saw a sudden look of disbelief and confusion on her face. She handed me the phone and on the other end was a paramedic, telling me that Michael was involved in a horrific car crash. His friend was driving at about 75 miles an hour and lost control of the car, hitting a tree, collapsing the passenger side of the car where Michael was sitting. I took a deep breath and asked the question that no parent should ever have to ask, "IS HE ALIVE?". The paramedic responded, yes, and that they were bringing him to the closest trauma center, which is about 20 minutes from our house. The accident itself had happened only a quarter of a mile from home.

Michael had been pinned in the car. After that, he was taken out by bystanders and laid on the cold roadway for over a half hour while waiting for an ambulance to arrive. Once at the hospital, it was discovered that Michael had 9 fractures: his nose, jaw, knee, wrist, the L5 in his spine, and four pelvic fractures. He also had internal bleeding, head lacerations and many teeth loosened due to the 58 pieces of dashboard wedged between his teeth and gums. When I first saw him in the emergency room, it took everything within me to hold it together, but I had to stay strong for him. He looked up at me and the doctor. His first words were "will I be able to play the guitar ever again". The first few days were critical and Michael was in Intensive Care; we sat, wondering if he would make it at all.

As friends and family gathered at the hospital, Michael began to slowly improve, but it was only the beginning of his long journey to recovery. After a few weeks, Michael was discharged from the hospital, but remained bed bound for months. The worst part for him was that he couldn't play the guitar due to all his injuries. At one point, Michael finally asked for his guitar. With his broken wrist and hand still in a cast, we were amazed at his request. At first, he could only play for very short periods of time, but you could see he was determined to not let his injuries stop him from pursuing his dreams. His passion for music gave him the strength and desire to get back on his feet as soon as possible.

Michael spent the next several months in a wheelchair. Unable to play guitar for long periods of time, he concentrated on his vocal talents and songwriting. He sang every day for 2 hours a day and developed his previously undiscovered amazing voice. Word got around Michael had a beautiful voice and was starting to play the guitar again. It wasn't too long after that when he received a phone call and was asked if he could play a few songs at a party in Westchester, New York. Although Michael was still in a wheelchair, he decided to do it anyway. I'm very happy to say that Michael hasn't stopped performing since.

As I reflect on that Christmas night in 2011, I believe it was truly a miracle that Michael survived that near fatal car accident. I believe he remained on this earth to share his gift of music. And without music in his life, I don't think he would have survived.

*Warren Golden*
*Mahopac, New York – U.S.A.*
*www.MichaelGolden.org*

# *Musical*

# *Potpourri*

Is it just us, or can you picture Fido crashing through the string quartet chasing after the stick?

## "Music & Love"

"Music is a lot like love in that they both require learning, listening and practice."

*6StringSarch*
*West Long Branch, New Jersey – U.S.A.*
*Former Guitar Player for Ray Charles*
*www.6StringSarch.com*

## "Getaway"

Music for me is a getaway from whatever the day brings, whatever you are stressing out about at the time. Music helps it all disappear, even if just for a little while. Just those 3 - 4 minutes of listening or performing your favorite song lets you open up and be yourself. That's what I really love most about music... there is nothing else that really does that for me.

*Alex B – Teen Pop Artist*
*Philadelphia, Pennsylvania – U.S.A.*
*www.AlexB.info*

> **When children learn music at an early age, their future has infinite possibilities.**

## *"Nothing to Fear"*

"At the age of 18, I simultaneously began teaching myself how to play guitar and write songs. I was sure, at the time, that I would keep my work secret and make music only for myself (which, I will add, was very therapeutic for an introvert such as myself!). A few months into my "secret project", a friend convinced me to perform some of my songs. After getting over my initial fears, I realized that the connection I was making to people through music was beginning to help get me out of my shell. Within a year, I was inspired enough to commit my life to writing and performing full time. Now, seven years later, I can confidently (and joyfully!) say that what music has given my life is unprecedented in every way.

There is nothing I have found like the feeling of connecting with people through music, sharing a deep understanding with strangers, in the hour of a show. When what I have written helps another in any way, I feel I have succeeded. That knowledge, alone, brings me joy and inspiration.

Music bridges the gap between people and removes the film of judgment, fear, anxiety and uncertainty between strangers who, otherwise, might not even make eye contact or acknowledge one another. It is a gift that reminds us that there is nothing to fear in one another, that we are all equal, that we are all the same."

*Aly Spaltro of Lady Lamb*
*Brunswick, Maine – U.S.A.*
*www.LadyLambJams.com*

## *"We ARE the Music"*

"What I love most about performing, is whenever I see a toddler stand up, and while bending his or her knees and moving themselves up and down, try to find the rhythm of the song I am playing. Despite the fact they can barely walk, let alone dance, they are demonstrating something ancient, inherent, instinctual and true... that we are the music and the music is us....and the two cannot be separated".

Viva La Musica!

*Andy Mason*
*Portales, New Mexico – U.S.A.*
*www.AndyMasonMusic.org*

## *"A Song In Your Heart"*

Wake up every morning with a song on your heart, and your day will be just a little bit brighter.

*Bonnie Thomas*
*Folsom, Pennsylvania – U.S.A.*

## *"We Remember"*

I was always self-taught on the keys, and one day at 16, I was trying out a new keyboard in a local music store. A man came up to me and asked if I studied music with anyone. When I said that I hadn't, he asked if I would like to check out the teaching studio downstairs. I said yes, and when he played the keyboard I was floored because of how good he was. He said that he liked the way I played, and asked if I ever thought of going to Berklee College of Music. I replied that I had dreamed of it, but never thought that I could be good enough for that. He said that he thought that I was, and that he could get me ready to pass the audition. That's exactly what he did. I passed the test and graduated from Berklee four years later in 1979. I have made a living as a full time musician ever since and see the benefits of music in young people's lives every day in my students.

On a solo gig, a few days after 9/11, I started to quietly play an instrumental piano version of "The Battle Hymn Of The Republic." What had been loud atmosphere just moments before, suddenly became an absolutely silent crowd with people crying about what had just happened in our lives as Americans. It was a very powerful musical moment for everyone in the room and one that I will never forget.

*Brian Maes*
*Lynn, Massachusetts – U.S.A.*
*www.BrianMaesMusic.com*
*Singer/Keyboardist/Songwriter & Producer*

## Music speaks when we cannot...

## *"Dear Music"*

I am a 15 year old singer from Philadelphia, and last year I was in a production of "School House Rock Live! Jr." at the Upper Darby Summer Stage. This was one of the biggest plays I've been in so far and felt very fortunate to be singing the "The Great American Melting Pot" solo. On opening night, there was almost a full house in a very large auditorium. All of my family and friends were going that night, so I was very excited for them to see me sing. As the play went on, everything was going great. We got big claps from the audience and everyone seemed to be loving the show. It was finally time for my solo; I got on stage, heard the music come on and then started to sing. As I was singing, I thought to myself "why does my microphone sound like it's not on?" I soon realized I was right. My microphone wasn't on. But you know what? I still kept going. I kept singing my heart out, even knowing that most of the people wouldn't be able to hear me. I just kept going, because the show must go on. As the song went on, one of my friends in the play ran out on stage and gave me a hand held microphone.

Once the microphones came on and everyone could hear me sing for the first time, the crowd went wild. As the song came to an end, the auditorium was flooded with applause and a standing ovation. I have never felt anything like that before; the feeling of being overwhelmed with emotion. I was so humbled and wanted to laugh, cry and smile all at the same time. The applause went on for what felt like years. What initially turned out to be one of the scariest moments in my young music career, ended up being one of the best times I've ever had.   Once you're on stage, you never know what will happen, so you just keep going and have fun!

p.s. Dear Music, I will never be able to thank you enough for always being there for me!

*Brooke Falls*
*Philadelphia, PA – USA*
*www.BrookeFalls.com*

## *"If You Can't Find the Right Words"*

One my favorite quotes has always been:   *"If you're trying to write a song and can't find the right words, you are not being honest enough yet."*     It helps me to finish songs whenever I think of that.

*Buddy Brown*
*Orlando, Florida – U.S.A.*
*www.BuddyBrownCountry.com*

## "He Ain't Heavy, He's My Brother"

One song changed my life. Thirty-six years ago, I had no intention of creating a serious commitment to anything. But after listening to The Hollies hit, "He Ain't Heavy, He's My Brother" at a fundraising dinner, I decided that I could make a contribution to children who needed caring adults in their lives by becoming a mentor.

I attended that fundraising dinner in my hometown of San Francisco in 1978 for a program called "Partners." The goal of the program was to pair caring adults with children already in the juvenile justice system for minor crimes. This was my introduction to the concept of one-to-one mentoring and "He Ain't Heavy, He's My Brother" was the group's theme song. Mentoring, said the organizers that night, can change a child's life. And they were planning to change one life at a time.

We were told that mentoring was a way to reduce the cycle of children who were incarcerated from graduating to the adult prison system. After that event, I contacted the program and offered to help in any way that I could, including becoming a mentor. Because the program was just being developed in the San Francisco Bay Area, I was asked if I could join the small group of fundraisers to spread the word and to help develop the program.

I worked as a volunteer for months, while keeping my day job as a writer. Although my professional background helped me in crafting program materials and contacting the media, I was also learning about developing a program from the ground up. Next, I joined the all-volunteer Board of Directors, to help officially manage the program. Finally, after we had hired some staff, I was interviewed and vetted as a potential mentor and matched with a 12 year old boy named Jim. He lived with his mother in a small apartment in a city on the San Francisco Peninsula. His teacher had approached the program because he was absent from school a few days each week. He had not been convicted of any crime, but his teacher was concerned about the choices he was making at a very young age.

By this time, I was working for a daily newspaper. I continued to promote the concept of mentoring as our local program was renamed Friends for Youth. Jim became a part of my weekly routine, picking him up each Wednesday and bringing him to my home to make dinner and review school work. I bought him an alarm clock and showed him how to use it. He agreed to carry a small notebook to school each day so his teacher could send me notes about his attendance, his academic performance and his behavior. Everything improved.

In addition to the weekly home visits, we shared adventures, such as ice skating at a local rink, and some holidays, such as joining my family for Easter brunch. We were matched for three years until his mother decided Jim should go live with an aunt and uncle in Georgia. It was bittersweet, knowing that his life going forward could be much better with a stable family, but I would miss our regular connections.

I continued to work as a newspaper reporter and kept my connection to Friends for Youth. Celebrating the organization's 20th anniversary included my helping to create the Friends for Youth Mentoring Institute. At about the same time, I received a wedding invitation from a Georgia address. My "little" Jim was getting married. I happily attended the ceremony and we got to talk about what our time together meant to him. He recalled the big events, like the holidays and special parties. But what he liked most, were the simple routines at home - feeding the animals, making dinner and practicing his spelling words. Just knowing that there was another style of life beyond what he had as a child was what he remembered the most.

Recently, I was reminded of a professor I once had

who was an important mentor for me during my college years. I realized that my work with Friends for Youth for all of these years, including my experiences with 12 to 14-year-old Jim, was just a way to "pay it forward." The song, "He Ain't Heavy, He's My Brother" talks about the long road many of us face when starting out, and never knowing where our path may eventually lead us. I will always associate this song with encouraging me to make a positive choice for me and for each child whose life can change by being matched with a mentor.

*Carol Blackman*
*San Francisco, California – U.S.A.*
*www.MoreToSayFromSF.com*
*Author of "Truth & Love: Finding the Soul of the Sixties"*

## *"Like an Old Friend"*

Music was always in my soul. I knew it as a child growing up, but could never explain how or why; I just knew that music would be part of my life, even before I could sing or play guitar. Without music, my life would have been so different. It was my purpose and, almost, my obsession at times. I can't think of any other job I could do and find the same happiness or satisfaction. For that, I know I am blessed and lead a very privileged life.

When I was just 13 years old, my two best friends (Neil and Paul) and I formed a band and it was so much fun. At the start, we could barely play, but as we progressed and did our first gigs, it felt amazing... like we were living a dream. I have never let go of that feeling and try to reach for it, still today, whenever I'm performing on stage.

My personal list of musical inspirations have been

many. There have been several Irish traditional songs that have influenced me. One, in particular, was the song "As I Roved Out" by a band called Planxty, a tune that still moves me every time I hear it. Being from Northern Ireland, Van Morrison was also a real hero. I was always very proud that a man from Belfast could do so much on the world stage. One night of live music I'll always remember, is when I met Damien Rice at a gig in Dublin, just as his debut album 'O' had gone to #1 in Ireland. That show was magical... everyone in the audience knew every word of every song and we all knew we were part of something very special that night.

There have been many people who have helped me along my journey. Michael Keeney was another musician who I formed a band with, and is one of the most talented individuals I know. It was so great creating music with Michael back then and we have continued to work together on many projects over the past 15 years. Linley Hamilton was the first music teacher who took me aside and gave me the confidence boost I needed when I was a young musician. He simply told me I was good enough to make it as a musician and, at the time, I really needed that encouragement.

Music has been a tremendous help to get me through a number of difficult times in my life. It's like an old friend that never leaves you, and one that you can always go back to, no matter what. Performing and, especially, creating music is amazing therapy. It's almost a form of meditation when you perform and writing songs is an incredible way to escape life and plug into your spiritual side. I have no doubt that music is my therapy every day of my life.

*Ciaran Gribbin*
*Belfast, Ireland*
*www.CiaranGribbin.com*

## *"We Can't All Be Playing"*

I grew up with all kinds of music. It surrounded me with joy and hope and love. Music to me, is a piece of my soul and I take it with me everywhere I go. It doesn't matter if I can carry a tune or even remember the right words; it is what it does to my self-esteem that holds the key to this little girl's dream.

Both sides of my family are very musical, however, you could say that my immediate family was an unusual bird. I grew up with Christian, Country and Classical music all around me, but none of my immediate family knew how to play a musical instrument with any expertise. It used to bother me when we would gather together at family reunions and we were the only ones not playing anything. When I expressed my feelings of inadequacy to my cousin Bruce, who plays string instruments, he simply replied, "Someone's got to listen and enjoy the music and let us know how we sound. We can't all be playing!" This simple statement made me very happy, and was in fact an epiphany; to realize that those of us listening were just as important to music as those who played and sang.

*Cindy Barry Strobel - Author*
*Kemp, Texas – U.S.A.*
*www.Reclaimed-Objects.tumblr.com*
*Excerpted from the soon to be published book:*
*"What Are Your Treasures"*

## *"Surf and Sound Make Beautiful Music"*

I always wanted to have music in my life. I cannot tell you why, but I just knew I would always need to be surrounded by sounds. I first picked up a guitar when I was seven years old; I can honestly say I didn't love it at first. At times, I even wanted to quit, but I kept with it. I started playing songs I liked and, slowly, my skills began to improve.

My deep passion for music didn't really come together, however, until I was probably 12 years old. It was then that I found an amazing connection between my love for surfing and music. They belong together. Once I combined my love of the ocean with my music, my songwriting started to flow.

I am fortunate to come from a loving family with a solid home life, and as a result, my music is rooted in a positive perspective. That good fortune has inspired me to give back to those less fortunate. Through the giveback programs and organizations I have had the pleasure to work with, it is clear to me, how much music can heal the damaged and inspire the lonely.

I've never allowed my age to get in the way of pursuing my passion... a music career. At the age of 14, I was discovered by Jason Mraz, a man and musician I admire very much. And for now, I am living my dream... playing music and surfing every day!

Music cures me and I hope that my music may help cure others.

*Cody Lovaas*
*Carlsbad, California – U.S.A.*
*www.CodyLovaas.com*

## *"My Most Treasured Instrument"*

My mum bought a small, upright piano for me when I was 8 years old and it is still the most treasured instrument I own. Even though it doesn't make as rich a sound as the more modern grand piano that I own and regularly play, this was the instrument that I first learned to play on. That upright piano opened up the wonderful world of music to me. Without the piano, I would never have had the opportunity to study music at school, then at music college and ultimately have a career as a composer. Being at the piano is where I'm most comfortable, whether writing or playing. It's the place where I feel most at home and at peace. I couldn't imagine my life without music and it's all because of the little upright piano that still takes pride of place in my living room.

*Debbie Wiseman MBE*
*Composer/Conductor*
*www.DebbieWiseman.co.uk*

## *"Music is My Smile"*

Music has always been in my heart and, since 1980, in my very soul... it is my smile!

Over the years, I have been inspired and influenced by many artists, but most especially the voices of Janis Joplin, Ella Fitzgerald, Georges Brassens and Francoise Hardy, just to name a few.

Meeting different people always influences me... nature influences me... silence influences me... the universe itself influences me!

Music is one of my best teachers. It has taught me to listen to the sounds of the universe... to people... to nature. It taught me to search within myself, to see what I am and what I am not. It has taught me to share, to express myself, to be sincere, and how to work with musicians and all people. Whenever I am on stage, music teaches me to give and how to receive.

Many have written to say how my songs and others have kept them alive. I think we all can agree that music is a very good anti-depressant... the sound of it is almost sacred and it's healing powers are practically without limit.

To make a difference or to inspire people, do what you love to do... for me, it will always be MUSIC!

*Desireless*
*Buis Les Baronnies, France*
*www.Desireless.net*

---

## No matter what...DON'T STOP the MUSIC!

---

## *"An Unconscious Process"*

Music has accompanied me through every time in my life. My experience has been, that difficult times in my life have helped me get through music.

My earliest personal musical influences were my mother, who was and is a virtuoso pianist, as well as my uncle, who played folk guitar and taught me my first chords. Later on, I had the good fortune of working with the amazing musicians in my first band, Evil Seed and then aligning with Rob Hyman and Rick Chertoff who, in some way, taught me everything I know.

I took piano lessons for a while when I was very young, but had neither the discipline, nor the patience, to progress very far. After learning my first guitar chords from my uncle, I became an autodidact; that is, I decided to teach myself guitar by painstakingly copying parts from the records I was listening to. I also taught myself mandolin, bass, saxophone, hurdy gurdy, harmonica and anything else I could lay my hands on. I never did participate in a school choir or ensemble, though I often wish that I had.

Along the way, there have been so many songs and artists that have shaped me throughout my life. I am of that generation who saw The Beatles on Ed Sullivan and felt the seismic shift of history first hand. I also got to see them live not once, but twice; yes, they really were that good. Other artists of note for me were Bob Dylan, The Who, Bruce Springsteen, Traffic, The Mahavishnu Orchestra, as well as lesser-known artists like The Blues Project, The Move and Autosalvage.

I've witnessed more touching situations involving music than I could ever list. Every performance where an artist is communicating with an audience is life-changing in some way. The opportunities I've had to meet people in unexpected circumstances, touch their lives and to be touched in so many ways are countless. Receiving letters and emails from people telling me how my songs have helped them through difficult times in their lives, having the opportunity to speak to students, veterans, people in every walk of life, enriches me at least as much as it touches them.

Music is absolutely my therapy. Writing songs is an unconscious process for me. It always tells me things about myself that I had either never known, or had known and forgotten. Music has also created the life I have. Things could have gone very differently. I'm sure I'd have been happy and successful as a doctor or a research scientist of some sort or maybe I would have found a home in the clergy (yes, the clergy, despite my feelings toward organized religion). But, music is what my life became and music is what it is and will be. For this, I am eternally grateful, because I get to (in some way) be all the above.

*Eric Bazilian*
*Philadelphia, Pennsylvania – U.S.A.*
*www.EricBazilian.com*

## "Optimum Results"

Music is the best cure for everything...For optimum results, listen to LIVE Music!

*Errol Desmond LeBlanc*
*Los Angeles, California – U.S.A.*
*www.Facebook.com/Errol.D.LeBlanc*

## "Every Piece of Human Emotion"

If I am speaking to parents who would like to create the next great classical concert pianist in the world, then please read no further... this will not pertain to you. For everyone else, I can only hope you will be the parents I was lucky enough to have, despite neither one achieving more than a high school education. There was brilliance in the way they handled my formative years. My parents possessed a knowledge of life that could not be taught. It all seemed so simple, yet that's where the beauty lies. They feared nothing, especially the music that was coming out of all those transistor and clock radios. They heard spirit and never tried to manipulate an outcome. I was never told what to like, or worse yet, "what not to like". They just left me alone.

So...Please...do NOT be "helicopter" parents for your children learning music. Music is NOT a sport... and should not be treated as such.

Music to me is, literally, every piece of human emotion transformed into a special sound and place.

Oh, and one more thing... I can confirm that one special person or teacher in your life, will absolutely make all the difference!

*Gary Mallaber*
*Los Angeles, California – U.S.A.*
*www.GaryMallaber.com*

## *"Hard to Say Goodbye"*

We are firm believer's that music is food for the soul. It has the power to create so many different emotions: both happy and sad feelings, and even has the ability to bring tears to your eyes. Music can also bring memories into your path, as it effortlessly takes you back to a moment in time.

We recently released a song called "Hard to Say Goodbye", which has the potential to help you remember all the different ways you've had to say goodbye. Whether you've had to say goodbye to a loved one you've lost, or perhaps to your parents and friends when you first moved away from home; music can make you feel better and can even be healing during these difficult times. There is no question that music is a pure blessing, and we are forever grateful to continue making music for all our wonderful fans!

*Great White*
*www.OfficialGreatWhite.com*

## "The Common Thread that Binds Us All"

My greatest inspiration was my high school band director, William Ledue. I played trumpet in the marching band in Coral Gables, Florida and, together, we had some amazing experiences. We went to Europe as a group, marched in the Orange Bowl and 100 of us were also in the concert band each year. I've never forgotten all the fun we had, and it's why I play music today.

To be able to create music is the greatest blessing of my life. I have been told countless times that my music has helped someone. I once received an email from someone who had just lost their job. It's two in the morning, and as they watched their family sleeping, they wondered how they were going to provide for them. They said that one of my songs came on the radio and gave them hope. Six months later, I met them at one of my concerts and was so happy to hear they had found work. They thanked me again for my music and said it really helped give them the power to continue on.

I have been told that my music has given comfort to

children as their parent passed away. I have been told by teachers, that my music on their iPod was the only thing that could calm one of their autistic students.

Music transcends language. There have been countries I've gone to where I have not been able to speak the language, but could communicate, just by playing my horn.

Songs are like planting seeds that grow into shade trees under which I will never sit. They are my children roaming throughout the world and extensions of my heart.

The notes of my horn speak far more eloquently of who I truly am than any words ever could. Music is the sound of the soul, the common thread that binds us all and reminds us of pure truth.

There is no war in music, only peace. Music is Love.

*Jeff Oster*
*Alameda, California – U.S.A.*
*www.JeffOster.com*
*www.RetsoRecords.com*

## *"Just One Song"*

I absolutely love music. When I was a teenager, I would often listen to the same song over and over again. At the time, I didn't understand the significance of this. Later in life, I began to realize that if I chose the right song, it would be like my own personal soundtrack. Hearing that one song would always make me feel great, like I was winning at everything in life. I've since learned that doing this actually puts our brains into an enlightened state; we become highly energized and our bodies will begin to vibrate differently. As a result, we feel great and begin to think and act differently. By continuing to listen to that same song, that elevated state leads us to believe that anything is possible.

For me, that one song is "Coming Around Again" by Carly Simon. I've probably listened to that song a thousand times, since I was 21 years old. Whenever I hear it, I visualize my goals all being met and accomplished. It is amazing how great that one song makes me feel. There are a few songs like that for me, but that would be my favorite. Now, whenever I want to get myself into that state of happiness and power, I listen to that song and the effect is almost instantaneous.

My iPod has room for thousands of songs, but I finally understand that I shouldn't use 1,000 songs...maybe just 1, 2 or 3 songs that make me feel better; songs that put me in the energized state I'm looking for. In today's world, I believe we have too many choices. I realized, that if I listen to a sad song, I will become sad. Why should I listen to that kind of song? The whole point is to not waste our time listening to many different songs when some are sad or depressing. I realize that not everyone will agree with this perspective, but for me, I am focusing on songs that put my mind, my brain in that elevated state that I am reaching for. Each one of us should choose one song that would be like the climax of a movie; our own personal movie that gives us that "Rocky at the top of the Art Museum steps" feeling. I now coach people to go with the idea that selecting songs should be analogous to Steve Jobs' initial design of the iPhone. Stay with simplicity, not so many choices, and the end result will be much better.

*Luis Souza*
*Londrina, Brazil*
*www.FeelBetterOnAir.com*

## *"In Tune with Life"*

Music is just like a life medicine to me. Without it, my mind is in a very dark place. I've been playing piano since I was 11 years old, self-taught and have never stopped. The more you practice what you love, the more emotions you unlock from your body. Music has allowed me to be "in tune" with life and all it's beauty and meaning. It's simply the best therapy there is.

*Mike Kalombo*
*Democratic Republic of the Congo / Tennessee – U.S.A.*
*So So Def / Kalombo  Records*
*www.SoundCloud.com/MikeKalombo*
*www.Instagram.com/MikeKalombo*
*www.Twitter.com/MikeKalombo*

## *"How I Got Back to Music"*

This is a true story of twists and turns and how music returned to be a major joy in my life.  When I was in fourth grade, there was a "talent" contest in our classroom every week. And, every week, I'd walk to the front of the room and sing a song that I had learned. It got to the point that the other kids in the class got sick of seeing me up there each week. But, I didn't care. Every week I'd be up there with another song.

In the summer between fourth and fifth grade, my father died, by suicide. After that, I became withdrawn and not very assertive. I also began to develop a lisp that I'm sure was emotionally based. I completely lost interest in music, as well as, a lot of other things. The school put me in the school chorus, which I tried to quit soon after, but the staff wouldn't let me.

Several years later, I was attending a summer church youth leadership week at King's College. I was walking down the dorm hall, when one of the college counselors put his arm around me and said, "Oh, I see you're going to choir practice". I wasn't, but not being very assertive, I went along anyway. Well, as it turned out, I loved it. And that was the beginning of my returning to music. I then joined the church choir, which I participated in until near the end of college.

At the end of my senior year at college, I had to take a couple of courses in the summer before I could graduate. I stayed in a dorm during that time and there was another guy I knew there who played guitar and sang. While in his room, I asked if I could "play" his guitar. I plucked the high "'E'" string, going up the fret board with one finger and said to myself, "Oh, so this is how it works". After college, I got married and we lived in an apartment in West Philadelphia. My sister-in-law later moved into the same building and she had a classical guitar that she didn't play. I asked if I could borrow it to learn a few chords and accompany myself, just for my own enjoyment.

The first real songbook I bought was a book of Phil Ochs songs. He became a real influence in my music. In the introduction to the book he said, "I hope this book will inspire some readers to try their hand at songwriting. You'll never know how good you might be without a few honest attempts. I think many potentially good songwriters have been still-born by their own inhibitions". I kept his words in my mind and, 6 years later, wrote my first song. I've since stopped counting, but I've probably written over 300 songs since.

It was a few years later, but I finally got up the nerve to go to an open mic and sing. It was a great experience and I've never looked back. That open mic occurred about 35 years ago. Since that time, music has taken me on many journeys. I've hosted both a radio and cable TV show showcasing songwriters, managed 3 performing songwriters, produced two concert series, booked several venues, hosted more open mics than I wish to remember and have produced and hosted an internet radio program and two internet TV programs. I have also personally performed at a number of venues, including the Philadelphia Folk Festival in 1997, which was absolutely a musical highlight in my life.

One especially rewarding experience I had with music was when I was employed as a social worker in a psychiatric hospital. I worked in an all-women's facility, which had two units; one of which treated women with severe psychotic symptoms. Occasionally, I would take my guitar into work and sing songs for the patients. Most of the songs were songs people would know such as "Home on The Range", or "Swinging on A Star". One day, I played for patients on the unit with the women experiencing psychotic symptoms. As I was playing, one particular woman had her head down, with little expression on her face and, basically, not paying attention. She most likely attended the group so she would not miss out on her next smoke break (attendance was required to be eligible for things like a smoke break). At one point, I announced to the group that I was going to sing an original song called "Willie The Bipolar Polar Bear". The song is a funny song, but with a message. As I sang the song, the woman with her head down slowly began to raise it up, then smiled and slowly began to laugh. This may have been the only time she smiled and laughed during her entire hospital stay. As a songwriter and performer, touching someone on an emotional level like this is what moves us to continue to create and perform.

Finding a way back to music after the tragedy of losing my father at the age of 9, has made all the difference in my life and, as a result, has helped others along the way. It's often funny how things happen. If that counselor at the summer retreat had not put his arm around me and dragged me to that choir practice, my life may have turned out quite differently. I may have never had all the amazing and wonderful musical experiences I have enjoyed throughout my life and still continue to enjoy today.

*Ray Naylor*
*Folcroft, Pennsylvania – U.S.A.*
*www.RayNaylor.net*

## *"Why Music Matters To Me"*

My brother and I were born to a low income, mixed race family of Japanese and Irish American parents. To top it off, my mother suffered from schizophrenia, I was the smallest one in my class (my mom was 4"8") and my brother and I grew up without any other family (my dad left when I was just 4 years old). After moving to the U.S., my mother became a pioneering member of the Soka Gakkai International, a religious organization that promotes peace, culture and education. So, being a small, poor, fatherless, "half breed", Buddhist child with a "weird mom", made my life more than a little challenging. I was frequently bullied about my ethnicity, size, religion, home life... you name it, I got teased for it.

As part of the Soka Gakkai, my mother participated in SGI World Peace Culture Festivals, and my earliest memories of music are from attending these events. In fact, it's the music that I remember most about them. There were brass bands, fife & drum corps, steel drum groups, drill dancers (color guard), traditional Japanese dancers and different choruses. Even though I was very young, I remember thinking to myself that, someday, I wanted to sing, dance or play an instrument just like them.

When I was in elementary school, I signed up to learn the violin. My mom said it was okay but after a few weeks, I had to return the violin to the school... she told me I was disturbing the neighbors. Boy, was I crushed! So, I didn't get to play an instrument, but I did enjoy our regular music classes throughout the rest of the school year. I always looked forward to music, as it was my most favorite subject of all. During those younger years, my mom also enrolled my brother and I in a summer arts and crafts program. The camps were run by high schoolers and college kids, and that's when I was really exposed to music. I remember hearing artists like Elton John, Captain 'n Tennille, Debby Boone, the Bay City Rollers, Elvis Presley, and many more. The camp leaders always played music from their transistor radios... and I loved it!

When I moved on to middle school, I joined the winter chorus. The night of our first concert, I remember feeling so sick & nervous about walking up on the stage - actually, scared to death and feeling like I was going to faint. But, once we were up there and actually singing, I felt much better. Unfortunately, I was not able to continue with chorus after that, because my mother said we couldn't afford it. I'm guessing it had something to do with the cost of attire and transportation. So, again, it was my music class that brought me happiness. My music teacher, Mr. Richard Poole, was the coolest! That was when I first learned of The Beatles. Mr. Poole had all kinds of cool rock posters on his walls and he taught us "cool" songs.

He was my favorite teacher all throughout my school years, although I never told him and wish I had.

High school is when I started listening more to music. Some of my favorite 80's artists & bands were Duran Duran, Bryan Adams, Culture Club, Bon Jovi, Journey, Hall & Oates, Prince, The Go-Go's, The Bangles, Phil Collins, Level 42, Toto, The Human League, Bananarama, The Thompson Twins, Billy Idol and, of course, Madonna (just to name a few). By that time, my brother had a record player. Whenever going out, he would always say, "Don't go in my room and DON'T touch my record player". So, do you know what I did? Yup, I played the heck out of those records! I used to pretend I was Barry Manilow, Shaun Cassidy or Chaka Kahn and belted out one song after another.

It's hard to believe, but even in high school, I was bullied about the same things I was teased about in elementary school. The one thing I always looked forward to was going home to my little clock radio... I turned it on and pretty much played it all the time. Music is the one thing I could always count on... it would help me forget the bullies, forget how poor we were, my mom's chemical imbalance and it just made me feel better. While in high school, I earned money by babysitting, which allowed me to go to under 21 clubs with my friends, where we danced the night away. One of the clubs we went to held dance contests. The winners received tickets to appear on a locally filmed television show called "Dancin' On Air". Guess who (with her friends) won a contest? Yup! We ended up appearing on the show several times and I loved every minute of it! Dancing was such a great way to release stress and have fun.

During the 80's, I also had the wonderful opportunity to participate in several World Peace Culture Festivals. I was in the fife & drum corps, where I played the piccolo (well, sort of, but that's a story for another time) for parades in Washington, D.C. and Philadelphia. I also performed in festivals with the drill dancers at Madison Square Gardens in NY and also at The Spectrum in Philadelphia. All of these events were performed in front of thousands of people. Despite being terribly shy and not very talented, I did quite well...because it was music!

Fast forward to the 1990's. I had an opportunity to attend an event held by a local radio station where a pen pal from high school was performing. Although he sent me tickets to his shows during high school, they were far away and I was never able to attend. I contacted Trish Merelo (one of the radio station DJ's) and told her my pen pal story. She thought it was great and was going to let him know I was coming to see him perform. That night, I finally got to meet my old pen pal, Tommy Page. Turns out Tommy had become quite successful and some may remember his songs "I'll Be Your Everything" and "A Shoulder to Cry On". I credit Tommy for, indirectly, leading me to the next chapter in my life. That same night, I met the person who would end up becoming my very best friend. This person was there to write an article for Out On The Town, an entertainment publication still in circulation today in the Philadelphia area. We developed a great friendship and have been best friends ever since. Eighteen months after we met, we were married and share 4 wonderful children together The one person in the world, who brightens my life every day (with or without music) and is the love of my life, is Vincent James...my co-author of this wonderfully inspiring book "88+ Ways Music Can Change Your Life".

All through the years, Vincent has been involved in music to some degree. He managed bands, organized and promoted shows, started the Philadelphia Songwriter's Association, taught piano & guitar, co-wrote with other artists, put out several CD's and created LoveSongs.com, along with Keep Music Alive. When our children were younger, it was difficult for me to be involved, although I took care of some of the administrative tasks. I mainly focused on raising our family. As the children have gotten older, I find myself happily involved in music again. I am very proud to be a part of Keep Music Alive and helping to promote the importance of music

Although all our children are creative, two of them are involved in music to some degree. Our oldest daughter, Priscilla, spent 9 years in chorus and is now in her 6th year of marching band. There were days when she practiced in the hot summer sun (nearly 100 degrees)10 hours a day, 5 days a week for 2 weeks straight (notoriously known as "band camp")... in addition to all the other practices held throughout the summer. There were times during the football season when it was so cold, I thought her fingers would fall off. Priscilla would be totally exhausted, but still managed to get good grades. Between Priscilla, Vincent, me and our youngest daughter Ana (who got dragged to all the competitions and football games), MANY hours were spent practicing, moving props, attending pre-show performances, working the concession stand, preparing hot meals for the band kids, traveling to and from competitions, etc. Priscilla will tell you that the most exciting times for her, were when they got to perform down Disney World's "Main Street U.S.A" and coming in the top three during 3 out of 4 years in the Cavalcade of Bands Championship competitions. I realized through all this, how truly valuable the marching band experience was for Priscilla. She learned a lot about patience, sacrifice, teamwork and made many new friends in the process. Priscilla is now in her college marching band, and had the incredible opportunity to perform in this past year's Macy's Thanksgiving Day Parade in NY. When Priscilla was in her high school's Chamber Choir, she also got to perform at The White House in Washington, D.C. Again, this another a once in a lifetime experience made possible by music.

And her little sister, Ana, who got dragged around to all those events for 4 years? She decided to try color guard her freshman year and experienced an amazing run, as the marching band was undefeated the entire season. Then for the first time in over 30 years, her high school placed 1st in the Cavalcade of Bands Championships American Open Division. Ana is now in her 7th year of chorus, has taken guitar & keyboarding classes in school, and is currently teaching herself violin.

After my mother suffered a stroke in October 2013, I began researching the therapeutic benefits of music. My mom's hospital was an hour away, so on my daily drives there and back, I always had the radio on... to help keep my spirits up. I also began playing music via my smartphone for my mom. Sometimes it was mediation music, other times it was Japanese style music (she was originally from Okinawa, Japan). I would even play 80's music. I played music when she was awake and while she slept... not constantly, but on and off. One day, my mom's physical therapist came in the room and heard the music playing. He was ecstatic! He said he wished more families researched the benefits of music and its effect on stroke patients. He commended me for my efforts and said, "believe it or not, it really does make a difference" and thanked me for taking an active role in my mother's rehabilitation. A few months later, I received a CD from my uncle in Okinawa with music from back when my mom was in her 20's and 30's. The moment I started playing it for her, she burst out crying. I immediately turned off the music. She whispered "No, I like it", because it reminded her of her younger days. I put the music back on and let it play. My mom has since passed away and my dear Vincent played a beautiful instrumental piece entitled "Kiyoko is Free to Fly" for her memorial service. It is one of the most beautiful, emotion evoking songs I have ever heard (even though there are no lyrics) and will be forever grateful to Vincent for this very special song he dedicated for my mom.

I now have a confession: I can't sing... I can't play an instrument... I can't even read music. But, do you know what I can do? I can SUPPORT MUSIC! I can help promote the importance of music in education, healing and making us happier human beings. If you ask me, that's pretty great! When I'm in the car with the radio playing, I sing my heart out! When my voice is cracking and totally off key (always), my kids give me crazy looks and put the windows up. One day, when I was singing along to a tune in the van, our youngest son Dave said to me "Who sings that song?" I said, "Journey". He said "Let's keep it that way". I cracked up laughing! What can I say... I LOVE MUSIC!

*Joann Pierdomenico*
*Philadelphia, Pennsylvania – U.S.A.*
*Co-Founder Keep Music Alive & LoveSongs.com*

**To share your inspirational music story,
please visit us at www.KeepMusicAlive.org**

# INDEX

6StringSarch - *Music & Love* .................................196
Adam Ezra w/Bruce Fredericks - *Remembering You Today* .............3
Alan Segal - *The Jazz Sanctuary* ...........................147
Alex B - *Getaway* ................................196
Aly Spaltro of Lady Lamb - *Nothing to Fear* ...............197
Andre Maranhao - *One Note at a Time* .....................89
Andy Mason - *We ARE the Music* .............................198
Ann Kelly - *I Truly Could Not Live a Day* ..................147
Audra Mclaughlin - *Never Give Up!* .........................7
Audrey Landers - *Music = Emotion* .........................9

Baran - *3 Kinds of People* .............................11
Bill Champlin - *The Living Years* ...........................149
Billy Steinberg - *Like A Virgin* ...........................12
Bluesman Jay Gullo - *Best Education I Ever Received* .........91
Bobby Hart & Glenn Ballantyne - *Anyone Here Play the Banjo?* .......94
Bobby Kimball - *Living Your Life for Happiness* .............15
Bonnie Thomas - *A Song In Your Heart* ....................198
Bonnie Warren - *Thanks Mom* .............................17
Brian Maes - *We Remember* .............................199
Bronsen Bloom - *Making Mom Happy Again* .................18
Brooke Falls - *Dear Music* ...........................200
Buddy Brown - *If You Can't Find the Right Words* .............201

Carol Blackman - *He Ain't Heavy, He's My Brother* ...........202
Chris D'Antonio - *Who Sings That Song?* .....................97
Chris McDermott - *Music Will Never Give Up on Us* ...........149
Ciaran Gribbin - *Like an Old Friend* .....................204
Cindy Barry Strobel - *We Can't All Be Playing* .............206
Cody Lovaas - *Surf and Sound Make Beautiful Music* .........207
Connie Kerbs - *The Amazing Avah Grace* .....................19
Craig Snyder - *Keep Your Ears Open* .....................123

# INDEX

Dalton Cyr - *A Whisper Heard Around The World*........................152
Darcy Donavan - *My Guardian Angel* .......................................153
David Charles - *Unforgettable*.....................................................98
Debbie Wiseman - *My Most Treasured Instrument* ......................208
Derek Anthony Wilson - *Music Saved Me from Myself*...................24
Desireless - *Music is My Smile*.................................................208
Dr. Deb Carlin - *We're All in This Together* ...............................155
Elise Hofmann - *Play Your Own Therapy* ..................................158
Eric Bazilian - *An Unconscious Process*....................................209
Eric Jacobsen - *The Better You Get, The More You'll Enjoy It*........160
Erin Carere - *A Divine Gift From the Universe* .............................26
Errol Desmond LeBlanc - *For Optimum Results*...........................211

Fred Mollin - *Standing on the Shoulders*.....................................28
Gary Alexander - *The Path of a Professional Musician*...................31
Gary Mallaber - *Every Piece of Human Emotion* .........................211
Grace Otley - *The Biggest Reward*............................................162
Great White - *Hard to Say Goodbye*...........................................212
Gregg Hammond - *Saved by the Guitar* ......................................34
Hank Alviani - *The Decision Chair*..............................................36
Howard Fields - *The World of Harry Chapin* ................................99

Jack Pearson - *To All Purple Tree Trunks* .................................164
Jana Mashonee  - *Together for Just One Night*............................39
Jasmine Mya Yedra - *HOME* ...................................................129
Jay Gruska - *I Don't Believe in Plan B* .......................................41
Jeff Oster - *The Common Thread that Binds Us All* .....................213
Jessica Lynn - *Connecting From the Heart* ..................................43
JKELL - *Never Believe Them*.....................................................45
Joann Pierdomenico - *Why Music Matters to Me*.........................219
Joey James - *If You Don't Dream Big, Why Dream At All*...............45
Jordan White - *It's Not All Unicorns and Rainbows* ......................47
Judy Pancoast - *Maybe It's You* ................................................49
Julia Zane - *Singing for Baby*....................................................165

# INDEX

Katherine Dines - *The Power to Heal*.........................................166

Kelsey Coan - *Don't Give Up* ...................................................50

Kevin Vieira - *Birth of an Artist* ...............................................53

Khim Teoh - *Dorothy Cho: Warrior of Hope*..............................125

Krista Hughes & Eve Bare - *Kids for the Blues -*...........................58

Kristin Smedley - *Best and Most Beautiful Things in Life*.................61

Leon Jordan, Sr - *Changing the Course of History*.......................101

Lisa Sniderman - *Music is My Lifeline & I Can't Stop Creating* .......168

Luis Souza - *Just One Song* ...................................................214


Marcy Holub - *Keep Music Alive*...............................................133

Mark King - *The Power of Music*...............................................173

Matthew Keith - *How Marching Band Changed My Life at Age 40!*..135

Melissa Polinar - *Above Water*...................................................63

Michel Rubini - *Feel the Magic in Your Life* ...............................102

Miguel Sague - *Music Brought My Mother Back to Me* .................174

Mike Kalombo - *In Tune with Life*..............................................216

Mini Thin - *Breaking Down* .......................................................65

Nick Ambrosino - *I Teach People, Not Pianos* ...........................137


Pat DiCesare - *Hard Days, Hard Nights* ...................................106

Patricia Shih - *A Hidden Star* ..................................................139

Pete Shand - *A Quiet, Driving Force Inside of Me* .......................176

Peter P. Carli II - *An Open Letter to All School Superintendents*.....141

Phyllis Chapell - *Therapy for the Performer Too*..........................178

Ray Naylor - *How I Got Back to Music* .....................................216

Rick Wakeman - *The Greatest Gift One Could Ever Give* ..............65

Rob Hyman - *There's Always a Song* ........................................110

Rob Parissi - *Classical Fab-Four Inspires Some Funky Music*........113

Rose Kingsley - *What I Did for Love* .........................................114

Ryan Weaver - *In Honor of My Brothers*......................................66

# INDEX

Sara Flatow - *Marching Beyond Halftime* ...................................179

Sara Spicer - *Heaven's Gate* ...............................................182

Siedah Garrett - *Man in the Mirror* ............................................68

Simon Kirke - *When Words Fail, Music Speaks* .............................70

Skip Denenberg - *Million to One* ...........................................117

Steve Kurtz - *On the Mic* ....................................................119

Suzanne Gorman - *How I Found the Real Me* ............................184

Suzi Shelton - *Music Lifts Us, When Nothing Else Can* .................186

Taylor Abrahamse - *You Get What You Give* ...............................72

The Battersbys - *A Day to Remember at Claremont Elementary* ....122

Theresa Shoup - *Penny Shouts It Out!* .......................................76

Valerie West - *Every Note and Lyric* .........................................80

Vanessa Carlton - *Music is Magic* ............................................80

Veronica Kole - *Forever Gone But Never Forgotten* ....................188

Victoria De Mare - *No Matter What, Write a Song About It* ............190

Warren Golden - *Will I Be Able to Play the Guitar Ever Again?* ......191

Wolfgang Gowin - *Hop & Pull* ...............................................81

Yosmar Salazar-Márquez Vinson - *It Takes a Village* ...................83

Ziba Shirazi - *The Gift of Music* ..............................................86

# "88+ Ways Music" Current Beneficiaries

**The Mr. Holland's Opus Foundation** keeps music alive in our schools by donating musical instruments to under-funded music programs nationwide, giving economically-disadvantaged youth access to the many benefits of music education, helping them to be successful students, and inspiring creativity and expression through playing music. *www.MHOPUS.org*

**The Spirit of Harmony** is Todd Rundgren's philanthropic organization that nurtures the study of music through special events, public information, mentoring, advocacy, social entrepreneurship, and strategic partnerships. Our work focuses on instrument-based music education, beginning at as early an age as possible, for a substantial length of time (minimum two years, and minimum four hours per week). We base our focus on research done on the benefits of music education. *www.SpiritOfHarmony.org*

**Guitars in the Classroom** provides free music integration classes for educators and school staff working with children of all ages in educational settings. We show teachers how to make music, lead music for learning and how to write songs with students in order to enhance and deepen their learning experience in every subject area. Participants also learn how to select or create songs that fit into the lessons they plan to teach. *www.GuitarsInTheClassroom.org*

# *"KEEP MUSIC ALIVE"*

## *Some ways you can help keep music alive:*

- Support music education in your community – Let your local politicians and school board know just how important music and art education is for your children AND for our collective future.

- Support up and coming artists and local venues that still offer live music. Bring your children out to events that feature music. Let them hear live music themselves and see how these experiences will help positively shape your child's development and future.

- If music is not currently offered in your schools, find alternate ways to introduce music education to your children, whether it's outside music schools, private teachers and even Youtube offers a wealth of free tutorials where you can learn how to play almost any instrument under the sun.

# For more information and resources, please visit www.KeepMusicAlive.org

44504498R00144

Made in the USA
Middletown, DE
09 June 2017